MOONWALK

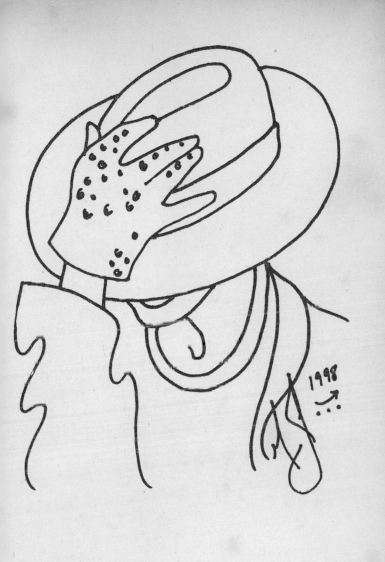

MOONWALK

By

Michael Jackson

Heinemann · Mandarin

A Mandarin Paperback

MOONWALK

ISBN 0 7493 0000 0

A CIP catalogue record for this book
is available from the British Library

First published in Great Britain 1988
by William Heinemann Ltd
This edition published 1989
by Heinemann · Mandarin
81 Fulham Road, London SW3 6RB
Copyright © 1988 by Michael Jackson

Reproduced, printed and bound in Great Britain by
Hazell Watson & Viney Limited
Member of BPCC plc
Aylesbury, Bucks, England

This book is dedicated to

F R E D   A S T A I R E

What can one say about Michael Jackson? He is one of the world's most acclaimed entertainers, an innovative and exciting songwriter whose dancing seems to defy gravity and has been heralded by the likes of Fred Astaire and Gene Kelly.

His public is perhaps unaware of the extent of his dedication to his craft. Restless, seldom satisfied, he is a perfectionist who is constantly challenging himself.

To many people Michael Jackson seems an elusive personality, but to those who work with him, he is not. This talented artist is a sensitive man, warm, funny, and full of insight. Michael's book, *Moonwalk*, provides a startling glimpse of the artist at work and the artist in reflection.

—*Jacqueline Kennedy Onassis*

When I want to discover something, I begin by reading up everything that has been done along that line in the past —that's what all the books in the library are for. I see what has been accomplished at great labor and expense in the past. I gather the data of many thousands of experiments as a starting point and then I make thousands more. The three essentials to achieve anything worthwhile are, first, hard work; second, stick-to-it-iveness; third, common sense.

—*Thomas Edison*

When the real music comes to me—the music of the spheres, the music that surpasseth understanding—that has nothing to do with me 'cause I'm just the channel. The only joy for me is for it to be given to me and transcribe it. Like a medium. Those moments are what I live for.

—*John Lennon*

MOONWALK

CHAPTER

ONE

JUST KIDS
WITH A DREAM

've always wanted to be able to tell stories, you know, stories that came from my soul. I'd like to sit by a fire and tell people stories—make them see pictures, make them cry and laugh, take them *unywhere* emotionally with something as deceptively simple as words. I'd like to tell tales to move their souls and transform them. I've always wanted to be able to do that. Imagine how the great writers must feel, knowing they have that power. I sometimes feel I *could* do it. It's something I'd like to develop. In a way, songwriting uses the same skills, creates the emotional highs and lows, but the story is a sketch. It's quicksilver. There are very few books written on the art of storytelling, how to grip listeners, how to get a group of people together and amuse them. No costumes, no makeup, no nothing, just you and your voice, and your powerful ability to take them anywhere, to transform their lives, if only for minutes.

As I begin to tell my story, I want to repeat what I usually say to people when they ask me about my earliest days with the Jackson 5: I was so little when we began to work on our music that I really don't remember much about it. Most people have the luxury of careers that start when they're old enough to know exactly what they're doing and why, but, of course, that wasn't true of me. They remember everything that happened to them, but I was only five years old. When you're a show business child, you really don't have the maturity to understand a great deal of what is going on around you. People make a lot of decisions concerning your life when you're out of the room. So here's what I remember. I remember singing at the top of my voice and dancing with real joy and working too hard for a child. Of course, there are many details I don't remember at all. I do remember the Jackson 5 really taking off when I was only eight or nine.

I was born in Gary, Indiana, on a late summer night in 1958, the seventh of my parents' nine children. My father, Joe Jackson, was born in Arkansas, and in 1949 he married my mother, Katherine Scruse, whose people came from

Alabama. My sister Maureen was born the following year and had the tough job of being the oldest. Jackie, Tito, Jermaine, LaToya, and Marlon were all next in line. Randy and Janet came after me.

A part of my earliest memories is my father's job working in the steel mill. It was tough, mind-numbing work and he played music for escape. At the same time, my mother was working in a department store. Because of my father, and because of my mother's own love of music, we heard it all the time at home. My father and his brother had a group called the Falcons who were the local R&B band. My father played the guitar, as did his brother. They would do some of the great early rock 'n' roll and blues songs by Chuck Berry, Little Richard, Otis Redding, you name it. All those styles were amazing and each had an influence on Joe and on us, although we were too young to know it at the time. The Falcons practiced in the living room of our house in Gary, so I was raised on R&B. Since we were nine kids and my father's brother had eight of his own, our combined numbers made for a huge family. Music was what we did for entertainment and those times helped keep us together and kind of encouraged my father to be a family-oriented man. The Jackson 5 were born out of this tradition—we later became the Jacksons —and because of this training and musical tradition, I moved out on my own and established a sound that is mine.

I remember my childhood as mostly work, even though I *loved* to sing. I wasn't *forced* into this business by stage parents the way Judy Garland was. I did it because I enjoyed it and because it was as natural to me as drawing a breath and exhaling it. I did it because I was *compelled* to do it, not by parents or family, but by my own inner life in the world of music.

There were times, let me make that clear, when I'd come home from school and I'd only have time to put my books down and get ready for the studio. Once there, I'd sing until late at night, until it was past my bedtime, really. There was a park across the street from the Motown studio, and I can remember looking at those kids playing games. I'd just stare at them in wonder—I couldn't imagine such freedom, such a carefree life—and wish more than anything that I had that kind of freedom, that I could walk away and be like them. So there were sad moments in my childhood. It's true for any child star. Elizabeth Taylor told me she felt the same way. When you're young and you're working, the world can seem awfully unfair. I wasn't forced to be little Michael the lead singer—I did it and I loved it—but it was hard work. If we were doing an album, for example, we'd go off to the studio after school and I might or might not get a snack. Sometimes there just wasn't time. I'd come home, exhausted, and it'd be eleven or twelve and past time to go to bed.

So I very much identify with anyone who worked as a child. I know how they struggled, I know what they sacrificed. I also know what they learned. I've learned that it becomes more of a challenge as one gets older. I feel old for some reason. I really feel like an old soul, someone who's seen a lot and experienced a lot. Because of all the years I've clocked in, it's hard for me to accept that I am only twenty-nine. I've been in the business for twenty-four years. Sometimes I feel like I should be near the end of my life, turning eighty, with people patting me on the back. That's what comes from starting so young.

When I first performed with my brothers, we were known as the Jacksons. We would later become the Jackson 5. Still later, after we left Motown, we would reclaim the Jacksons name again.

Every one of my albums or the group's albums has been dedicated to our mother, Katherine Jackson, since we took over our own careers and began to produce our own music. My first memories are of her holding me and singing songs like "You Are My Sunshine" and "Cotton Fields." She sang to me and to my brothers and sisters often. Even though she had lived in Indiana for some time, my mother grew up in Alabama, and in that part of the country it was just as common for black people to be raised with country and western music on the radio as it was for them to hear spirituals in church. She likes Willie Nelson to this day. She has always had a beautiful voice and I suppose I got my singing ability from my mother and, of course, from God.

Mom played the clarinet and the piano, which she taught my oldest sister, Maureen, whom we call Rebbie, to play, just as she'd teach my other older sister, LaToya. My mother knew, from an early age, that she would never perform the music she loved in front of others, not because she didn't have the talent and the ability, but because she was crippled by polio as a child. She got over the disease, but not without a permanent limp in her walk. She had to miss a great deal of school as a child, but she told us that she was lucky to recover at a time when many died from the disease. I remember how important it was to her that we got the sugar-cube vaccine. She even made us miss a youth club show one Saturday afternoon—*that's* how important it was in our family.

My mother knew her polio was not a curse but a test that God gave her to triumph over, and she instilled in me a love of Him that I will always have. She taught me that my talent for singing and dancing was as much God's work as a beautiful sunset or a storm that left snow for children to play in. Despite all the time we spent rehearsing and traveling, Mom would find time to take me to the Kingdom Hall of the Jehovah's Witnesses, usually with Rebbie and LaToya.

Years later, after we had left Gary, we performed on "The Ed Sullivan Show," the live Sunday night variety show where America first saw the Beatles, Elvis, and Sly and the Family Stone. After the show, Mr. Sullivan complimented and thanked each of us; but I was thinking about what he had said to me *before* the show. I had been wandering around backstage, like the kid in the Pepsi commercial, and ran into Mr. Sullivan. He seemed glad to see me and shook my hand, but before he let it go he had a special message for me. It was 1970, a year when some of the best people in rock were losing their lives to drugs and alcohol. An older, wiser generation in show business was unprepared to lose its very young. Some people had already said that I reminded them of Frankie Lymon, a great young singer of the 1950s who lost his life that way. Ed Sullivan may have been thinking of all this when he told me, *"Never* forget where your talent came from, that your talent is a gift from God."

I was grateful for his kindness, but I could have told him that my mother had never let me forget. I never had polio, which is a frightening thing for a dancer to think about, but I knew God had tested me and my brothers and sisters in other ways—our large family, our tiny house, the small amount of money we had to make ends meet, even the jealous kids in the neighborhood who threw rocks at our windows while we rehearsed, yelling that we'd never make it. When I think of my mother and our early years, I can tell you there are rewards that go far beyond money and public acclaim and awards.

My mother was a great provider. If she found out that one of us had an interest in something, she would encourage it if there was any possible way. If I developed an interest in movie stars, for instance, she'd come home with an armful of books about famous stars. Even with nine children she treated each of us like an only child. There isn't one of us who's ever forgotten what a hard worker and a great provider she was. It's an old story. Every child thinks *their* mother is the greatest mother in the world, but we Jacksons never lost that feeling. Because of Katherine's gentleness, warmth, and attention, I can't imagine what it must be like to grow up without a mother's love.

One thing I know about children is that if they don't get the love they need from their parents, they'll get it from someone else and cling to that person, a grandparent, anyone. We never had to look for anyone else with my mother around. The lessons she taught us were invaluable. Kindness, love, and consideration for other people headed her list. Don't hurt people. Never beg. Never freeload. Those were sins at our house. She always wanted us to *give*, but she never wanted us to ask or beg. That's the way she is.

I remember a good story about my mother that illustrates her nature. One day, back in Gary, when I was real little, this man knocked on everybody's door early in the morning. He was bleeding so badly you could see where he'd been around the neighborhood. No one would let him in. Finally he got to our door and he started banging and knocking. Mother let him in at once. Now, most people would have been too afraid to do that, but that's my mother. I can remember waking up and finding blood on our floor. I wish we could all be more like Mom.

The earliest memories I have of my father are of him coming home from the steel mill with a big bag of glazed doughnuts for all of us. My brothers and I could really eat back then and that bag would disappear with a snap of the fingers. He used to take us all to the merry-go-round in the park, but I was so young I don't remember that very well.

My father has always been something of a mystery to

me and he knows it. One of the few things I regret most is never being able to have a real closeness with him. He built a shell around himself over the years and, once he stopped talking about our family business, he found it hard to relate to us. We'd all be together and he'd just leave the room. Even today it's hard for him to touch on father and son stuff because he's too embarrassed. When I see that he is, I become embarrassed, too.

My father did always protect us and that's no small feat. He always tried to make sure people didn't cheat us. He looked after our interests in the best ways. He might have made a few mistakes along the way, but he always thought he was doing what was right for his family. And, of course, most of what my father helped us accomplish was wonderful and unique, especially in regard to our relationships with companies and people in the business. I'd say we were among a fortunate few artists who walked away from a childhood in the business with anything substantial—money, real estate, other investments. My father set all these up for us. He looked out for both our interests and his. To this day I'm so thankful he didn't try to take all our money for himself the way so many parents of child stars have. Imagine stealing from your own children. My father never did anything like that. But I still don't know him, and that's sad for a son who hungers to understand his own father. He's still a mystery man to me and he may always be one.

What I got from my father wasn't necessarily God-given, though the Bible says you reap what you sow. When we were coming along, Dad said that in a different way, but the message was just as clear: You could have all the talent in the world, but if you didn't prepare and plan, it wouldn't do you any good.

Joe Jackson had always loved singing and music as much as my mother did, but he also knew there was a world beyond Jackson Street. I wasn't old enough to remember his band, the Falcons, but they came over to our house to rehearse on weekends. The music took them away from their jobs at the steel mill, where Dad drove a crane. The Falcons would play all over town, and in clubs and colleges around northern Indiana and Chicago. At the rehearsals at our house, Dad would bring his guitar out of the closet and plug it into the amp he kept in the basement. Everyone would be set up and the music would begin. He'd always loved rhythm and blues and that guitar was his pride and joy. The closet where the guitar was kept was considered an almost sacred place. Needless to say, it was off-limits to us kids. Dad didn't go to Kingdom Hall with us, but both Mom and Dad knew that music was a way of keeping our family together in a neighborhood where gangs recruited kids my brothers' ages. The three oldest boys would always have an excuse to be around when the Falcons came over. Dad let them think they were being given a special treat by being allowed to listen, but he was actually eager to have them there.

Tito watched everything that was going on with the greatest interest. He'd taken saxophone in school, but he could tell his hands were big enough to grab the chords and slip the riffs that my father played. It made sense that he'd catch on, because Tito looked so much like my father that we all expected him to share Dad's talents. The extent of the resemblance was scary as he got older. Maybe my father noticed Tito's zeal because he laid down rules for all my brothers: No one was to touch the guitar while he was out. Period.

Therefore, Jackie, Tito, and Jermaine were careful to see that Mom was in the kitchen when they "borrowed" the guitar. They were also careful not to make any noise while removing it. They would then go back to our room and put on the radio or the little portable record player so they could play along. Tito would hoist the guitar onto his belly as he sat on the bed and prop it up. He took turns with Jackie and Jermaine, and they'd all try the scales they were learning in school as well as try to figure out how to get the "Green Onions" part they'd hear on the radio.

By now I was old enough to sneak in and watch if I promised not to tell. One day Mom finally caught them, and we were all worried. She scolded the boys, but said she wouldn't tell Dad as long as we were careful. She knew that guitar was keeping them from running with a bad crowd and maybe getting beat up, so she wasn't about to take away anything that kept them within arm's reach.

Of course, something had to give sooner or later, and one day a string broke. My brothers panicked. There wasn't time to get it repaired before Dad came home, and besides, none of us knew how to go about getting it fixed. My brothers never figured out what to do, so they put the guitar back in the closet and hoped fervently that my father would think it broke by itself. Of course, Dad didn't buy that, and he was furious. My sisters told me to stay out of it and keep a low profile. I heard Tito crying after Dad found out and I went to investigate, of course. Tito was on his bed crying when Dad came back and motioned for him to get up. Tito was scared, but my father just stood there, holding his favorite guitar. He gave Tito a hard, penetrating look and said, "Let me see what you can do."

My brother pulled himself together and started to play a few runs he had taught himself. When my father saw how well Tito could play, he knew he'd obviously been practicing and he realized that Tito and the rest of us didn't treat his favorite guitar as if it were a toy. It became clear to him that what had happened had been only an accident. At this point my mother stepped in and voiced her enthusiasm for our musical ability. She told him that we boys had talent and he should listen to us. She kept pushing for us, so one day he began to listen and he liked what he heard. Tito, Jackie, and Jermaine started rehearsing together in earnest. A couple of years later, when I was about five, Mom pointed out to my father that I was a good singer and could play the bongos. I became a member of the group.

About then my father decided that what was happening in his family was serious. Gradually he began spending less time with the Falcons and more with us. We'd just woodshed together and he'd give us tips and teach us techniques on the guitar. Marlon and I weren't old enough to play, but we'd watch when my father rehearsed the older boys and we were learning when we watched. The ban on using Dad's guitar still held when he wasn't around, but my brothers loved using it when they could. The house on Jackson Street was bursting with music. Dad and Mom had paid for music lessons for Rebbie and Jackie when they were little kids, so they had a good background. The rest of us had music class and band in the Gary schools, but no amount of practice was enough to harness all that energy.

The Falcons were still earning money, however infrequent their gigs, and that extra money was important to us. It was enough to keep food on the table for a growing family but not enough to give us things that weren't necessary. Mom was working part-time at Sears, Dad was still working the mill job, and no one was going hungry, but I think, looking back, that things must have seemed like one big dead end.

One day Dad was late coming home and Mom began to get worried. By the time he arrived, she was ready to give him a piece of her mind, something we boys didn't mind witnessing once in a while just to see if he could take it like he dished it out, but when he poked his head through the door, he had a mischievous look on his face and he was hiding something behind his back. We were all shocked when he produced a gleaming red guitar, slightly smaller than the one in the closet. We were all hoping this meant we'd get the old one. But Dad said the new guitar was Tito's. We gathered around to admire it, while Dad told Tito he had to share it with anyone who would *practice*. We were not to take it to school to show it off. This was a serious present and that day was a momentous occasion for the Jackson family.

Mom was happy for us, but she also knew her husband. She was more aware than we of the big ambitions and plans he had for us. He'd begun talking to her at night after we kids were asleep. He had dreams and those dreams didn't stop with one guitar. Pretty soon we were dealing with *equipment*, not just gifts. Jermaine got a bass and an amp. There were shakers for Jackie. Our bedroom and living room began to look like a music store. Sometimes I'd hear Mom and Dad fight when the subject of money was brought up, because all those instruments and accessories meant having to go without a little something we needed each week. Dad was persuasive, though, and he didn't miss a trick.

We even had microphones in the house. They seemed like a real luxury at the time, especially to a woman who was trying to stretch a very small budget, but I've come to realize that having those microphones in our house wasn't just an attempt to keep up with the Joneses or anyone else in amateur night competitions. They were there to help us prepare. I saw people at talent shows, who probably sounded great at home, clam up the moment they got in front of a microphone. Others started screaming their songs like they wanted to prove they didn't need the mikes. They didn't have the advantage that we did—an advantage that only experience can give you. I think it probably made some people jealous because they could tell our expertise with the mikes gave us an edge. If that was true, we made so many sacrifices—in free time, schoolwork, and friends—that no one had the right to be jealous. We were becoming very good, but we were working like people twice our age.

While I was watching my older brothers, including Marlon on the bongo drums, Dad got a couple of young guys named Johnny Jackson and Randy Rancifer to play trap drums and organ. Motown would later claim they were our cousins, but that was just an embellishment from the P R people, who wanted to make us seem like one big family. We had become a real band! I was like a sponge, watching everyone, and trying to learn everything I could. I was totally absorbed when my brothers were rehearsing or playing at charity events or shopping centers. I was most fascinated when watching Jermaine because he was the singer at the time and he was a big brother to me—Marlon was too close to me in age for that. It was Jermaine who would walk me to kindergarten and whose clothes would be handed down to me. When he did something, I tried to imitate him. When I was successful at it, my brothers and Dad would laugh, but when I began singing, they listened. I was singing in a baby voice then and just imitating sounds. I was so young I didn't know what many of the words meant, but the more I sang, the better I got.

I always knew how to dance. I would watch Marlon's moves because Jermaine had the big bass to carry, but also because I could keep up with Marlon, who was only a year older than me. Soon I was doing most of the singing at home and preparing to join my brothers in public. Through our rehearsals, we were all becoming aware of our particular strengths and weaknesses as members of the group and the shift in responsibilities was happening naturally.

Our family's house in Gary was tiny, only three rooms really, but at the time it seemed much larger to me. When you're that young, the whole world seems so huge that a little room can seem four times its size. When we went back to Gary years later, we were all surprised at how tiny that house was. I had remembered it as being large, but you could take five steps from the front door and you'd be out the back. It was really no bigger than a garage, but when we lived there it seemed fine to us kids. You see things from such a different perspective when you're young.

Our school days in Gary are a blur for me. I vaguely

remember being dropped off in front of my school on the first day of kindergarten, and I clearly remember hating it. I didn't want my mother to leave me, naturally, and I didn't want to be there.

In time I adjusted, as all kids do, and I grew to love my teachers, especially the women. They were always very sweet to us and they just loved me. Those teachers were so wonderful; I'd be promoted from one grade to the next and they'd all cry and hug me and tell me how much they hated to see me leave their classes. I was so crazy about my teachers that I'd steal my mother's jewelry and give it to them as presents. They'd be very touched, but eventually my mother found out about it, and put an end to my generosity with her things. That urge that I had to give them something in return for all I was receiving was a measure of how much I loved them and that school.

One day, in the first grade, I participated in a program that was put on before the whole school. Everyone of us in each class had to do something, so I went home and discussed it with my parents. We decided I should wear black pants and a white shirt and sing "Climb Ev'ry Mountain" from *The Sound of Music*. When I finished that song, the reaction in the auditorium overwhelmed me. The applause was thunderous and people were smiling; some of them were standing. My teachers were crying and I just couldn't believe it. I had made them all happy. It was such a great feeling. I felt a little confused too, because I didn't think I had done anything special. I was just singing the way I sang at home every night. When you're performing, you don't realize what you sound like or how you're coming across. You just open your mouth and sing.

Soon Dad was grooming us for talent contests. He was a great trainer, and he spent a lot of money and time working with us. Talent is something that God gives to a person, but our father taught us how to cultivate it. I think we also had a certain instinct for show business. We loved to perform and we put everything we had into it. He'd sit at home with us every day after school and rehearse us. We'd perform for him and he'd critique us. If you messed up, you got hit, sometimes with a belt, sometimes with a switch. My father was real strict with us—real strict. Marlon was the one who got in trouble all the time. On the other hand, I'd get beaten for things that happened mostly outside rehearsal. Dad would make me so mad and hurt that I'd try to get back at him and get beaten all the more. I'd take a shoe and throw it at him, or I'd just fight back, swinging my fists. That's why I got it more than all my brothers combined. I would fight back and my father would kill me, just tear me up. Mother told me I'd fight back even when I was very little, but I don't remember that. I do remember running under tables to get away from him, and making him angrier. We had a turbulent relationship.

Most of the time, however, we just rehearsed. We *always* rehearsed. Sometimes, late at night, we'd have time to play games or play with our toys. There might be a game of hide-and-go-seek or we'd jump rope, but that was about it. The majority of our time was spent working. I clearly remember running into the house with my brothers when my father came home, because we'd be in big trouble if we weren't ready to start rehearsals on time.

Through all this, my mother was completely supportive. She had been the one who first recognized our talent and she continued to help us realize our potential. It's hard to imagine that we would have gotten where we did without her love and good humor. She worried about the stress we were under and the long hours of rehearsal, but we wanted to be the best we could be and we really loved music.

Music was important in Gary. We had our own radio stations and nightclubs, and there was no shortage of people who wanted to be on them. After Dad ran our Saturday afternoon rehearsals, he'd go see a local show or even drive all the way to Chicago to see someone perform. He was always watching for things that could help us down the road. He'd come home and tell us what he'd seen and who was doing what. He kept up on all the latest stuff, whether it was a local theater that ran contests we could enter or a Cavalcade of Stars show with great acts whose clothes or moves we might adapt. Sometimes I wouldn't see Dad until I got back from Kingdom Hall on Sundays, but as soon as I ran into the house he'd be telling me what he'd seen the night before. He'd assure me I could dance on one leg like James Brown if I'd only try *this* step. There I'd be, fresh out of church, and back in show business.

We started collecting trophies with our act when I was six. Our lineup was set; the group featured me at second from the left, facing the audience, Jermaine on the wing next to me, and Jackie on my right. Tito and his guitar took stage right, with Marlon next to him. Jackie was getting tall and he towered over Marlon and me. We kept that setup for contest after contest and it worked well. While other groups we'd meet would fight among themselves and quit, we were becoming more polished and experienced. The people in Gary who came regularly to see the talent shows got to know us, so we would try to top ourselves and surprise them. We didn't want them to begin to feel bored by our act. We knew change was always good, that it helped us grow, so we were never afraid of it.

Winning an amateur night or talent show in a ten-minute, two-song set took as much energy as a ninety-minute concert. I'm convinced that because there's no room for mistakes, your concentration burns you up inside more on one or two songs than it does when you have the luxury of twelve or fifteen in a set. These talent shows were our professional education. Sometimes we'd drive hundreds of miles to do one song or two and hope the crowd wouldn't be against us because we weren't local talent. We were competing against people of all ages and skills, from drill teams to comedians to other singers and dancers like us. We had to grab that audience and keep it. Nothing was left to chance, so clothes, shoes, hair, *every-thing* had to be the way Dad planned it. We really looked amazingly professional. After all this planning, if we performed the songs the way we rehearsed them, the awards would take care of themselves. This was true even when we were in the Wallace High part of town where the neighborhood had its own performers and cheering sections and we were challenging them right in their own backyards. Naturally, local performers always had their own very loyal fans, so whenever we went off our turf and onto someone else's, it was very hard. When the master of ceremonies held his hand over our heads for the "applause meter," we wanted to make sure that the crowd knew we had given more than anyone else.

As players, Jermaine, Tito, and the rest of us were under tremendous pressure. Our manager was the kind who reminded us that James Brown would *fine* his Famous Flames if they missed a cue or bent a note during a performance. As lead singer, I felt I—more than the others—couldn't afford an "off night." I can remember being onstage at night after being sick in bed all day. It was hard to concentrate at those times, yet I knew all the things my brothers and I had to do so well that I could have performed the routines in my sleep. At times like that, I had to remind myself not to look in the crowd for someone I knew, or at the emcee, both of which can distract a young performer. We did songs that people knew from the radio or songs my father knew were already classics. If you messed up, you *heard* about it because the fans knew those songs and they knew how they were supposed to sound. If you were going to change an arrangement, it needed to sound *better* than the original.

We won the citywide talent show when I was eight with our version of the Temptations' song "My Girl." The contest was held just a few blocks away at Roosevelt High.

From Jermaine's opening bass notes and Tito's first guitar licks to all five of us singing the chorus, we had people on their feet for the whole song. Jermaine and I traded verses while Marlon and Jackie spun like tops. It was a wonderful feeling for all of us to pass that trophy, our biggest yet, back and forth between us. Eventually it was propped on the front seat like a baby and we drove home with Dad telling us, "When you do it like you did tonight they can't *not* give it to you."

We were now Gary city champions and Chicago was our next target because it was the area that offered the steadiest work and the best word of mouth for miles and miles. We began to plan our strategy in earnest. My father's group played the Chicago sound of Muddy Waters and Howlin' Wolf, but he was open-minded enough to see that the more upbeat, slicker sounds that appealed to us kids had a lot to offer. We were lucky because some people his age weren't that hip. In fact, we knew musicians who thought the sixties sound was beneath people their age, but not Dad. He recognized great singing when he heard it, even telling us that he saw the great doo-wop group from Gary, the Spaniels, when they were stars not that much older than we. When Smokey Robinson of the Miracles sang a song like "Tracks of My Tears" or "Ooo, Baby Baby," he'd be listening as hard as we were.

The sixties didn't leave Chicago behind musically. Great singers like the Impressions with Curtis Mayfield, Jerry Butler, Major Lance, and Tyrone Davis were playing all over the city at the same places we were. At this point my father was managing us full-time, with only a part-time shift at the mill. Mom had some doubts about the soundness of this decision, not because she didn't think we were good but because she didn't know anyone else who was spending the majority of his time trying to break his children into the music business. She was even less thrilled when Dad told her he had booked us as a regular act at Mr. Lucky's, a Gary nightspot. We were being forced to spend our weekends in Chicago and other places trying to win an ever-increasing number of amateur shows, and these trips were expensive, so the job at Mr. Lucky's was a way to make it all possible. Mom was surprised at the response we were getting and she was very pleased with the awards and the attention, but she worried about us a lot. She worried about me because of my age. "This is quite a life for a nine-year-old," she would say, staring intently at my father.

I don't know what my brothers and I expected, but the nightclub crowds weren't the same as the Roosevelt High crowds. We were playing between bad comedians, cocktail organists, and strippers. With my Witness upbringing, Mom was concerned that I was hanging out with the wrong people and getting introduced to things I'd be better off learning much later in life. She didn't have to worry; just one look at some of those strippers wasn't going to get me *that* interested in trouble—certainly not at nine years old! That was an awful way to live, though, and it made us all the more determined to move on up the circuit and as far away from that life as we could go.

Being at Mr. Lucky's meant that for the first time in our lives we had a whole show to do—five sets a night, six nights a week—and if Dad could get us something out of town for the seventh night, he was going to do it. We were working hard, but the bar crowds weren't bad to us. They liked James Brown and Sam and Dave just as much as we did and, besides, we were something extra that came free with the drinking and the carrying on, so they were surprised and cheerful. We even had some fun with them on one number, the Joe Tex song "Skinny Legs and All." We'd start the song and somewhere in the middle I'd go out into the audience, crawl under the tables, and pull up the ladies' skirts to look under. People would throw money as I scurried by, and when I began to dance, I'd scoop up all the dollars and coins that had hit the floor earlier and push them into the pockets of my jacket.

I wasn't really nervous when we began playing in

clubs because of all the experience I'd had with talent show audiences. I was always ready to go out and perform, you know, just *do* it—sing and dance and have some fun.

We worked in more than one club that had strippers in those days. I used to stand in the wings of this one place in Chicago and watch a lady whose name was Mary Rose. I must have been nine or ten. This girl would take off her clothes and her panties and throw them to the audience. The men would pick them up and sniff them and yell. My brothers and I would be watching all this, taking it in, and my father wouldn't mind. We were exposed to a lot doing that kind of circuit. In one place they had cut a little hole in the musicians' dressing room wall that also happened to act as a wall in the ladies' bathroom. You could peek through this hole, and I saw stuff I've never forgotten. Guys on that circuit were so wild, they did stuff like drilling little holes into the walls of the ladies' loo all the time. Of course, I'm sure that my brothers and I were fighting over who got to look through the hole. "Get outta the way, it's *my* turn!" Pushing each other away to make room for ourselves.

Later, when we did the Apollo Theater in New York, I saw something that really blew me away because I didn't know things like that existed. I had seen quite a few strippers, but that night this one girl with gorgeous eyelashes and long hair came out and did her routine. She put on a *great* performance. All of a sudden, at the end, she took off her wig, pulled a pair of big oranges out of her bra, and revealed that she was a hard-faced guy under all that makeup. That blew me away. I was only a child and couldn't even conceive of anything like that. But I looked out at the theater audience and they were *going* for it, applauding wildly and cheering. I'm just a little kid, standing in the wings, watching this crazy stuff.

I was blown away.

As I said, I received quite an education as a child. More than most. Perhaps this freed me to concentrate on other aspects of my life as an adult.

31

One day, not long after we'd been doing successfully in Chicago clubs, Dad brought home a tape of some songs we'd never heard before. We were accustomed to doing popular stuff off the radio, so we were curious why he began playing these songs over and over again, just one guy singing none too well with some guitar chords in the background. Dad told us that the man on the tape wasn't really a performer but a songwriter who owned a recording studio in Gary. His name was Mr. Keith and he had given us a week to practice his songs to see if we could make a record out of them. Naturally, we were excited. We wanted to make a record, any record.

We worked strictly on the sound, ignoring the dancing routines we'd normally work up for a new song. It wasn't as much fun to do a song that none of us knew, but we were already professional enough to hide our disappointment and give it all we could. When we were ready and felt we had done our best with the material, Dad got us on tape after a few false starts and more than a few pep talks, of course. After a day or two of trying to figure out whether Mr. Keith liked the tape we had made for him, Dad suddenly appeared with more of his songs for us to learn for our first recording session.

Mr. Keith, like Dad, was a mill worker who loved music, only he was more into the recording and business end. His studio and label were called Steeltown. Looking back on all this, I realize Mr. Keith was just as excited as we were. His studio was downtown, and we went early one Saturday morning before "The Road Runner Show," my favorite show at the time. Mr. Keith met us at the door and opened the studio. He showed us a small glass booth with all kinds of equipment in it and explained what various tasks each performed. It didn't look like we'd have to lean over any more tape recorders, at least not in this studio. I put on some big metal headphones, which came

halfway down my neck, and tried to make myself look
ready for anything.

As my brothers were figuring out where to plug in
their instruments and stand, some backup singers and a
horn section arrived. At first I assumed they were there to
make a record after us. We were delighted and amazed
when we found out they were there to record with us. We
looked over at Dad, but he didn't change expression. He'd
obviously known about it and approved. Even then people knew not to throw Dad surprises. We were told to
listen to Mr. Keith, who would instruct us while we were
in the booth. If we did as he said, the record would take
care of itself.

After a few hours, we finished Mr. Keith's first song.
Some of the backup singers and horn players hadn't made
records either and found it difficult, but they also didn't
have a perfectionist for a manager, so they weren't used
to doing things over and over the way we were. It was at
times like these that we realized how hard Dad worked to
make us consummate professionals. We came back the
next few Saturdays, putting the songs we'd rehearsed during the week into the can and taking home a new tape of
Mr. Keith's each time. One Saturday, Dad even brought
his guitar in to perform with us. It was the one and only
time he ever recorded with us. After the records were

pressed, Mr. Keith gave us some copies so that we could sell them between sets and after shows. We knew that wasn't how the big groups did it, but everyone had to start someplace, and in those days, having a record with your group's name on it was quite something. We felt very fortunate.

That first Steeltown single, "Big Boy," had a mean bass line. It was a nice song about a kid who wanted to fall in love with some girl. Of course, in order to get the full picture, you have to imagine a skinny nine-year-old singing this song. The words said I didn't want to hear fairy tales any more, but in truth I was far too young to grasp the real meanings of most of the words in these songs. I just sang what they gave me.

When that record with its killer bass line began to get radio play in Gary, we became a big deal in our neighborhood. No one could believe we had our own record. *We* had a hard time believing it.

After that first Steeltown record, we began to aim for all the big talent shows in Chicago. Usually the other acts would look me over carefully when they met me, because I was so little, particularly the ones who went on after us. One day Jackie was cracking up, like someone had told him the funniest joke in the world. This wasn't a good sign right before a show, and I could tell Dad was worried he was going to screw up onstage. Dad went over to say a word to him, but Jackie whispered something in his ear and soon Dad was holding his sides, laughing. I wanted to know the joke too. Dad said proudly that Jackie had overheard the headlining act talking among themselves. One guy said, "We'd better not let those Jackson 5 cut us tonight with that midget they've got."

I was upset at first because my feelings were hurt. I thought they were being mean. I couldn't help it that I was the shortest, but soon all the other brothers were cracking up too. Dad explained that they weren't laughing at me. He told me that I should be proud, the group was talking trash because they thought I was a grown-up posing as a child like one of the Munchkins in *The Wizard of Oz.* Dad said that if I had those slick guys talking like the neighborhood kids who gave us grief back in Gary, then we had Chicago on the run.

We still had some running of our own to do. After we played some pretty good clubs in Chicago, Dad signed us up for the Royal Theater amateur night competition in town. He had gone to see B. B. King at the Regal the night he made his famous live album. When Dad gave Tito that sharp red guitar years earlier, we had teased him by thinking of girls he could name his guitar after, like B. B. King's Lucille.

We won that show for three straight weeks, with a new song every week to keep the regular members of the audience guessing. Some of the other performers complained that it was greedy for us to keep coming back, but they were after the same thing we were. There was a policy that if you won the amateur night three straight times, you'd be invited back to do a *paid* show for thousands of people, not dozens like the audiences we were playing to in bars. We got that opportunity and the show was headlined by Gladys Knight and the Pips, who were breaking in a new song no one knew called "I Heard It Through the Grapevine." It was a heady night.

After Chicago, we had one more big amateur show we really felt we needed to win: the Apollo Theater in New York City. A lot of Chicago people thought a win at the Apollo was just a good luck charm and nothing more, but Dad saw it as much more than that. He knew New York had a high caliber of talent just like Chicago and he knew there were more record people and professional musicians in New York than Chicago. If we could make it in New York, we could make it anywhere. That's what a win at the Apollo meant to us.

Chicago had sent a kind of scouting report on us to New York and our reputation was such that the Apollo entered us in the "Superdog" finals, even though we hadn't been to any of the preliminary competitions. By this time, Gladys Knight had already talked to us about coming to Motown, as had Bobby Taylor, a member of the Vancouvers, with whom my father had become friendly. Dad had told them we'd be happy to audition for Motown, but that was in our future.

We got to the Apollo at 125th Street early enough to get a guided tour. We walked through the theater and stared at all of the pictures of the stars who'd played there, white as well as black. The manager concluded by showing us to the dressing room, but by then I had found pictures of all my favorites.

While my brothers and I were paying dues on the so-called "chitlin' circuit," opening for other acts, I carefully watched all the stars because I wanted to learn as much as I could. I'd stare at their feet, the way they held their arms, the way they gripped a microphone, trying to decipher what they were doing and why they were doing it. After studying James Brown from the wings, I knew every step, every grunt, every spin and turn. I have to say he would give a performance that would exhaust you, just wear you out emotionally. His whole physical presence, the fire coming out of his pores, would be phenomenal. You'd *feel* every bead of sweat on his face and you'd know what he was going through. I've never seen anybody perform like him. Unbelievable, really. When I watched somebody I liked, *I'd be there.* James Brown, Jackie Wilson, Sam and Dave, the O'Jays—they all used to really *work* an audience. I might have learned more from watching Jackie Wilson than from anyone or anything else. All of this was a very important part of my education.

We would stand offstage, behind the curtains, and watch everyone come off after performing and they'd be all sweaty. I'd just stand aside in awe and watch them walk by. And they would all wear these beautiful patent-leather shoes. My whole dream seemed to center on having a pair of patent-leather shoes. I remember being so heartbroken because they didn't make them in little boys' sizes. I'd go from store to store looking for patent-leather shoes and they'd say, "We don't make them that small." I was so sad because I wanted to have shoes that looked the way those stage shoes looked, polished and shining, turning red and orange when the lights hit them. Oh, how I wanted some patent-leather shoes like the ones Jackie Wilson wore.

Most of the time I'd be alone backstage. My brothers would be upstairs eating and talking and I'd be down in the wings, crouching real low, holding on to the dusty, smelly curtain and watching the show. I mean, I really did watch every step, every move, every twist, every turn, every grind, every emotion, every light move. That was my education and my recreation. I was always there when I had free time. My father, my brothers, other musicians, they all knew where to find me. They would tease me about it, but I was so absorbed in what I was seeing, or in remembering what I had just seen, that I didn't care. I remember all those theaters: the Regal, the Uptown, the Apollo—too many to name. The talent that came out of those places is of mythical proportions. The greatest education in the world is watching the masters at work. You couldn't teach a person what I've learned just standing and watching. Some musicians—Springsteen and U2, for example—may feel they got their education from the streets. I'm a performer at heart. I got mine from the stage.

Jackie Wilson was on the wall at the Apollo. The photographer captured him with one leg up, twisted, but not out of position from catching the mike stand he'd just whipped back and forth. He could have been singing a sad lyric like "Lonely Teardrops," and yet he had that audience so bug-eyed with his dancing that no one could feel sad or lonely.

Sam and Dave's picture was down the corridor, next to an old big-band shot. Dad had become friendly with Sam Moore. I remember being happily amazed that he was nice to me when I met him for the first time. I had been singing his songs for so long that I thought he'd want to box my ears. And not far from them was "The King of Them All, Mr. Dynamite, Mr. Please Please Himself," James Brown. Before he came along, a singer was a singer and a dancer was a dancer. A singer might have danced and a dancer might have sung, but unless you were Fred Astaire or Gene Kelly, you probably did one better than the other, especially in a live performance. But he changed all that. No spotlight could keep up with him when he skidded across the stage—you had to *flood* it! I wanted to be that good.

We won the Apollo amateur night competition, and I felt like going back to those photos on the walls and thanking my "teachers." Dad was so happy he said he could have *flown* back to Gary that night. He was on top of the world and so were we. My brothers and I had gotten straight A's and we were hoping we might get to skip a "grade." I certainly sensed that we wouldn't be doing talent shows and strip joints much longer.

In the summer of 1968 we were introduced to the music of a family group that was going to change our sound and our lives. They didn't all have the same last name, they were black and white, men and women, and they were

called Sly and the Family Stone. They had some amazing
hits over the years, such as "Dance to the Music," "Stand,"
"Hot Fun in the Summertime." My brothers would point
at me when they heard the line about the midget standing
tall and by now I'd laugh along. We heard these songs all
over the dial, even on the rock stations. They were a
tremendous influence on all of us Jacksons and we owe
them a lot.

After the Apollo, we kept playing with one eye on the
map and one ear to the phone. Mom and Dad had a rule
about no more than five minutes a call, but when we came
back from the Apollo, even five minutes was too long. We
had to keep the lines clear in case anyone from a record
company wanted to get in touch with us. We lived in fear
of having them get a busy signal. We wanted to hear from
one record company in particular, and if they called, we
wanted to answer.

While we waited, we found out that someone who
had seen us at the Apollo had recommended us to "The
David Frost Show" in New York City. We were going to be
on TV! That was the biggest thrill we'd ever had. I told
everyone at school, and told the ones who didn't believe
me twice. We were going to drive out there in a few days.
I was counting the hours. I had imagined the whole trip,

trying to figure out what the studio would be like and how it would be to look into a television camera.

I came home with the traveling homework my teacher had made up in advance. We had one more dress rehearsal and then we'd make a final song selection. I wondered which songs we'd be doing.

That afternoon, Dad said the trip to New York was canceled. We all stopped in our tracks and just stared at him.

We were shocked. I was ready to cry. We had been about to get our big break. How could they do this to us? What was going on? Why had Mr. Frost changed his mind? I was reeling and I think everyone else was, too. "I canceled it," my father announced calmly. Again we all stared at him, unable to speak. "Motown called." A chill ran down my spine.

I remember the days leading up to that trip with near-perfect clarity. I can see myself waiting outside Randy's first-grade classroom. It was Marlon's turn to walk him home, but we switched for today.

Randy's teacher wished me luck in Detroit, because Randy had told her we were going to Motown to audition. He was so excited that I had to remind myself that he didn't really know what Detroit was. All the family had

been talking about was Motown, and Randy didn't even
know what a city was. The teacher told me he was looking
for Motown on the globe in the classroom. She said that in
her opinion we should do "You Don't Know Like I Know"
the way she saw us do it at the Regal in Chicago when a
bunch of teachers drove over to see us. I helped Randy
put his coat on and politely agreed to keep it in mind—
knowing that we couldn't do a Sam and Dave song at a
Motown audition because they were on Stax, a rival label.
Dad told us the companies were serious about that kind of
stuff, so he wanted us to know there'd be no messing
around when we got there. He looked at me and said he'd
like to see his ten-year-old singer make it to eleven.

We left the Carrott Elementary School building for
the short walk home, but we had to hurry. I remember
getting anxious as a car swept by, then another. Randy
took my hand, and we waved to the crossing guard. I
knew LaToya would have to go out of her way tomorrow
to take Randy to school because Marlon and I would be
staying over in Detroit with the others.

The last time we played at the Fox Theater in Detroit,
we left right after the show and got back to Gary at five
o'clock in the morning. I slept in the car most of the way,
so going to school that morning wasn't as bad as it might
have been. But by the afternoon three o'clock rehearsal I

was dragging around like someone with lead weights for feet.

We could have left that night right after our set, since we were third on the bill, but that would have meant missing the headliner, Jackie Wilson. I'd seen him on other stages, but at the Fox he and his band were on a rising stage that moved up as he started his show. Tired as I was after school the next day, I remember trying some of those moves in rehearsal after practicing in front of a long mirror in the bathroom at school while the other kids looked on. My father was pleased and we incorporated those steps into one of my routines.

Just before Randy and I turned the corner onto Jackson Street, there was a big puddle. I looked for cars but there weren't any, so I let go of Randy's hand and jumped the puddle, catching on my toes so I could spin without getting the cuffs of my corduroys wet. I looked back at Randy, knowing that he wanted to do the things I did. He stepped back to get a running start, but I realized that it was a pretty big puddle, too big for him to cross without getting wet, so, being a big brother first and a dance teacher second, I caught him before he landed short and got wet.

Across the street the neighborhood kids were buying candy, and even some of the kids who were giving me a

hard time at school asked when we were going to Motown. I told them and bought candy for them and Randy,
too, with my allowance. I didn't want Randy to feel bad
about my going away.

As we approached the house I heard Marlon yell,
"Someone shut that door!" The side of our VW minibus
was wide open, and I shuddered, thinking about how cold
it was going to be on the long ride up to Detroit. Marlon
had beat us home and was already helping Jackie load the
bus with our stuff. Jackie and Tito got home in plenty of
time for once: They were supposed to have basketball
practice, but the winter in Indiana had been nothing but
slush and we were anxious to get a good start. Jackie was
on the high school basketball team that year, and Dad
liked to say that the next time we went to play in India-
napolis would be when Roosevelt went to the state cham-
pionships. The Jackson 5 would play between the evening
and morning games, and Jackie would sink the winning
shot for the title. Dad liked to tease us, but you never
knew what might happen with the Jacksons. He wanted
us to be good at many things, not just music. I think maybe
he got that drive from his father, who taught school. I
know my teachers were never as hard on us as he was, and
they were getting paid to be tough and demanding.

Mom came to the door and gave us the thermos and

the sandwiches she had packed. I remember her telling me not to rip the dress shirt she had packed for me after sewing it up the night before. Randy and I helped put some things in the bus and then went back into the kitchen, where Rebbie was keeping one eye on Dad's supper and the other on little Janet, who was in the high chair.

Rebbie's life was never easy as the oldest. We knew that as soon as the Motown audition was over, we'd find out if we had to move or not. If we did, she was going to move South with her fiancé. She always ran things when Mom was at night school finishing the high school diploma she was denied because of her illness. I couldn't believe it when Mom told us she was going to get her diploma. I remember worrying that she'd have to go to school with kids Jackie's or Tito's age and that they'd laugh at her. I remember how she laughed when I told her this and how she patiently explained that she'd be with other grown-ups. It was interesting having a mother who did home-work like the rest of us.

Loading up the bus was easier than usual. Normally Ronnie and Johnny would have come to back us up, but Motown's own musicians would be playing behind us, so we were going alone. Jermaine was in our room finishing some of his assignments when I walked in. I knew he

above My father and my mother.

left Imagine singing and
dancing at this age.

First Place Winners Of The Talent Search

THE JACKSON FIVE ..... Youthful musical aggregation who were First Place winners of the Annual Talent Search held last Sunday at Gilroy Stadium. The well attended and entertaining affair was Emceed by WWCA's popular Disc Jockey, Jesse Coopwood, who is well known for keeping the public entertained with his capers via the miles. Cherry, assisting Coopwood with the group of "Winners" is shown left in the photo. Proceeds from the affair will go toward a scholarship fund.

above My mother and Janet in Indiana.
below Johnny Jackson is playing the drums in this early publicity photograph.

top One of the early talent shows where we won a trophy.
middle Practicing after school.
lower Returning home to our small house in Gary after our success. The welcome was overwhelming.

left, top "Big Boy" was our first recorded song.

left At the NAACP Image Awards.

middle Performing together in the early days.

below My love of hats began long before the days of "Billie Jean"

left, top One of the many photo sessions we did with Motown.

centre Bill Cosby gives us the rules of love and baseball.

below right By this time the microphone had become a natural extension of my hand.

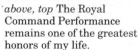

above, top The Royal
Command Performance
remains one of the greatest
honors of my life.

middle and right Berry was
closely involved in
everything we did,
including our appearance
on the Diana Ross TV
Special in 1971.

left With Berry Gordy and Suzanne de Passe.

left Working on *The E. T. Storybook* with Q and Steven Spielberg.

middle Jermaine joins the Jacksons on stage for the first time since the Jackson 5 days. A very special evening. Motown 25, 1983.

below Frank Dileo and I clown around for the camera.

bottom left At John Branca and Julia McArthur's wedding with Little Richard, who performed the ceremony.

HEARTBREAK HOTEL

Words and Music by MICHAEL JACKSON — Recorded by THE JACKSONS on Epic Records

left My friend Fred Astaire.

middle A visit to the White House.

below With Ola Ray in the "Thriller" video.

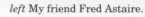

wanted to get them out of the way. He told me that we ought to take off for Motown by ourselves and leave Dad, since Jackie had taken driver's ed and was in possession of a set of keys. We both laughed, but deep down I couldn't imagine going without Dad. Even on the occasions when Mom led our after-school rehearsals because Dad hadn't come home from his shift on time, it was still like having him there because she acted as his eyes and ears. She always knew what had been good the night before and what had gotten sloppy today. Dad would pick it up from there at night. It seemed to me that they almost gave each other signals or something—Dad could always tell if we had been playing like we were supposed to by some invisible indication from Mom.

47

There was no long good-bye at the door when we left for Motown. Mom was used to our being away for days, and during school vacations. LaToya pouted a little because she wanted to go. She had only seen us in Chicago, and we had never been able to stay long enough in places like Boston or Phoenix to bring her back anything. I think our lives must have seemed pretty glamorous to her because she had to stay home and go to school. Rebbie had her hands full trying to put Janet to sleep, but she called good-bye and waved. I gave Randy a last pat on the head and we were off.

Dad and Jackie went over the map as we drove away, mostly out of habit, because we had been to Detroit before, of course. We passed Mr. Keith's recording studio downtown by City Hall as we made our way through town. We had done some demos at Mr. Keith's that Dad sent to Motown after the Steeltown record. The sun was going down when we hit the highway. Marlon announced that if we heard one of our records on WVON, it was going to bring us luck. We all nodded. Dad asked us if we remembered what WVON stood for as he nudged Jackie to keep quiet. I kept looking out the window, thinking about the possibilities that lay ahead, but Jermaine jumped in. "Voice of the Negro," he said. Soon we were calling roll all over the dial. "WGN—World's Greatest Newspaper." (The Chicago *Tribune* owned it.) "WLS—World's Largest Store." (Sears.) "WCFL . . ." We stopped, stumped. "Chicago Federation of Labor," Dad said, motioning for the thermos. We turned onto I-94, and the Gary station faded into a Kalamazoo station. We began flipping around, looking for Beatle music on CKLW from Windsor, Ontario, Canada.

I had always been a Monopoly fan at home, and there was something about driving to Motown that was a little like that game. In Monopoly you go around the board buying things and making decisions; the "chitlin' circuit" of theaters where we played and won contests was kind of like a Monopoly board full of possibilities and pitfalls. After all the stops along the way, we finally landed at the Apollo Theater in Harlem, which was definitely Park Place for young performers like us. Now we were on our way up Boardwalk, heading for Motown. Would we win the game or slide past Go with a long board separating us from our goal for another round?

There was something changing in me, and I could feel it, even shivering in the minibus. For years we'd make the drive over to Chicago wondering if we were good enough to ever get out of Gary, and we were. Then we took the drive to New York, certain that we'd fall off the edge of the earth if we weren't good enough to make it there. Even those nights in Philadelphia and Washington didn't reassure me enough to keep me from wondering if there wasn't someone or some group we didn't know about in New York who could beat us. When we tore it down at the Apollo, we finally felt that nothing could stand in our way. We were going to Motown, and nothing there was going to surprise us either. We were going to surprise them, just like we always did.

Dad pulled the typewritten directions out of the glove compartment and we pulled off the highway, passing the Woodward Avenue exit. There weren't many people on the streets because it was a school night for everybody else.

Dad was a little nervous about whether our accommodations would be okay, which surprised me until I realized the Motown people had picked the hotel. We weren't used to having things done for us. We liked to be our own bosses. Dad had always been our booking agent, travel agent, and manager. When he wasn't taking care of the arrangements, Mom was. So it was no wonder that even Motown managed to make Dad feel suspicious that *he* should have made the reservations, that he should have handled everything.

We stayed at the Gotham Hotel. The reservations had been made and everything was in order. There was a TV in our room, but all the stations had signed off, and with the audition at ten o'clock, we weren't going to get to stay up any later anyway. Dad put us right to bed, locked the door, and went out. Jermaine and I were too tired to even talk.

We were all up on time the next morning; Dad saw to that. But, in truth, we were just as excited as he was and hopped out of bed when he called us. The audition was unusual for us because we hadn't played in many places where they expected us to be professional. We knew it was going to be difficult to judge whether we were doing well. We were used to audience response whether we were competing or just performing at a club, but Dad had told us the longer we stayed, the more they wanted to hear.

We climbed into the VW, after cereal and milk at the coffee shop. I noticed they offered grits on the menu, so I knew there were a lot of Southern people who stayed there. We had never been to the South then and wanted to visit Mom's part of the country someday. We wanted to have a sense of our roots and those of other black people, especially after what had happened to Dr. King. I remember so well the day he died. Everyone was torn up. We didn't rehearse that night. I went to Kingdom Hall with Mom and some of the others. People were crying like they had lost a member of their own family. Even the men who were usually pretty unemotional were unable to control their grief. I was too young to grasp the full tragedy of the situation, but when I look back on that day now, it makes me want to cry—for Dr. King, for his family, and for all of us.

Jermaine was the first to spot the studio, which was known as Hitsville, U.S.A. It looked kind of run-down, which was not what I'd expected. We wondered who we might see, who might be there making a record that day. Dad had coached us to let him do all the talking. Our job was to perform like we'd never performed before. And that was asking a lot, because we always put everything into each performance, but we knew what he meant.

There were a lot of people waiting inside, but Dad said the password and a man in a shirt and tie came out to meet us. He knew each of our names, which astounded us. He asked us to leave our coats there and follow him. The other people just stared through us like we were ghosts. I wondered who they were and what their stories were. Had they traveled far? Had they been here day after day hoping to get in without an appointment?

When we entered the studio, one of the Motown guys was adjusting a movie camera. There was an area set up with instruments and microphones. Dad disappeared into one of the sound booths to talk to someone. I tried to pretend that I was at the Fox Theater, on the rising stage, and this was just business as usual. I decided, looking around, that if I ever built my own studio, I'd get a mike like the one they had at the Apollo, which rose out of the floor. I nearly fell on my face once running down those basement steps while trying to find out where it went when it slowly disappeared beneath the stage floor.

The last song we sang was "Who's Lovin' You." When

it ended, no one applauded or said a word. I couldn't stand not knowing, so I blurted, "How was that?" Jermaine shushed me. The older guys who were backing us up were laughing about something. I looked at them out of the corner of my eye. "Jackson Jive, huh?" one of them called out with a big grin on his face. I was confused. I think my brothers were too.

The man who had led us back said, "Thanks for coming up." We looked at Dad's face for some indication, but he didn't seem pleased or disappointed. It was still daylight out when we left. We took I-94 back to Gary, subdued, knowing there was homework to do for class tomorrow, wondering if that was all there was to that.

53

CHAPTER
TWO

THE
PROMISED LAND

We were jubilant when we learned we had passed the Motown audition. I remember Berry Gordy sitting us all down and saying that we were going to make history together. "I'm gonna make you the biggest thing in the world," he said, "and you're gonna be written about in history books." He really said that to us. We were leaning forward, listening to him, and saying, "Okay! Okay!" I'll never forget that. We were all over at his house, and it was like a fairy tale come true listening to this powerful, talented man tell us we were going to be very big. "Your first record will be a number one, your second record will be a number one, and so will your third record. Three number one records in a row. You'll hit the charts just as

Diana Ross and the Supremes did." This was almost un-
heard of in those days, but he was right; we turned around
and did just that. Three in a row.

So Diana didn't find us first, but I don't think we'll
ever be able to repay Diana properly for all she did for us
in those days. When we finally moved to Southern California, we actually lived with Diana and stayed with her for
more than a year on a part-time basis. Some of us lived
with Berry Gordy and some of us with Diana, and then we
would switch. She was so wonderful, mothering us and
making us feel right at home. She really helped take care
of us for at least a year and a half while my parents closed
up the Gary house and looked for a house we could all live
in here in California. It was great for us because Berry and
Diana lived on the same street in Beverly Hills. We could
walk up to Berry's house and then go back to Diana's.
Most of the time I'd spend the day at Diana's and the
night at Berry's. This was an important period in my life
because Diana loved art and encouraged me to appreciate it too. She took the time to educate me about it. We'd
go out almost every day, just the two of us, and buy pencils
and paint. When we weren't drawing or painting, we'd go
to museums. She introduced me to the works of the great
artists like Michelangelo and Degas and that was the start
of my lifelong interest in art. She really taught me a great

deal. It was so new to me and so exciting. It was really different from what I was used to doing, which was living and breathing music, rehearsing day in and day out. You wouldn't think a big star like Diana would take the time to teach a kid to paint, to give him an education in art, but she did and I loved her for it. I still do. I'm crazy about her. She was my mother, my lover, and my sister all combined in one amazing person.

Those were truly wild days for me and my brothers. When we flew to California from Chicago, it was like being in another country, another world. To come from our part of Indiana, which is so urban and often bleak, and to land in Southern California was like having the world transformed into a wonderful dream. I was uncontrollable back then. I was all over the place—Disneyland, Sunset Strip, the beach. My brothers loved it too, and we got into everything, like kids who had just visited a candy store for the first time. We were awestruck by California; trees had oranges and leaves on them in the middle of winter. There were palm trees and beautiful sunsets, and the weather was so warm. Every day was special. I would be doing something that was fun and wouldn't want it to end, but then I'd realize there was something else to do later that was going to be just as enjoyable and that I could look forward to just as much. Those were heady days.

One of the best parts of being there was meeting all the big Motown stars who had emigrated to California along with Berry Gordy after he moved from Detroit. I remember when I first shook Smokey Robinson's hand. It was like shaking hands with a king. My eyes lit up with stars, and I remember telling my mother that his hand felt as if it was layered with soft pillows. You don't think about the little impressions people walk away with when you're a star yourself, but the fans do. At least, I know I did. I mean, I walked around saying, "His hand is *so soft.*" When I think about it now, it sounds silly, but it made a big impression on me. I had shaken Smokey Robinson's hand. There are so many artists and musicians and writers I admire. When I was young, the people I watched were the *real* showmen—James Brown, Sammy Davis, Jr., Fred Astaire, Gene Kelly. A great showman touches everybody; that's the real test of greatness and these men have it. Like Michelangelo's work, it touches you, I don't care who you are. I am always excited when I get a chance to meet someone whose work has affected me in some way. Maybe I've read a book that has touched me deeply or made me think about things that I haven't focused on before. A certain song or style of singing can excite me or move me and become a favorite that I'll never tire of hearing. A picture or a painting can reveal a universe. In the same vein, an actor's performance or a collective performance can transform me.

In those days Motown had never recorded a kids' group. In fact the only child singer they had ever produced was Stevie Wonder. So Motown was determined that if they were going to promote kids, they'd promote the kind of kids who were good at more than just singing and dancing. They wanted people to like us because of who we were, not just because of our records. They wanted us to set an example by sticking to our schoolwork and being friendly to our fans, reporters, and everyone who came into contact with us. This wasn't hard for us because our mother had raised us to be polite and considerate. It was second nature. Our only problem with schoolwork was that once we became well known, we couldn't go to school because people would come into our classrooms through the windows, looking for an autograph or a picture. I was trying to keep up with my classes and not be the cause of disruptions, but it finally became impossible and we were given tutors to teach us at home.

During this period a lady named Suzanne de Passe was having a great effect on our lives. She worked for Motown, and it was she who trained us religiously once we moved to L.A. She also became a manager for the Jackson 5. We lived with her occasionally, ate with her, and even played with her. We were a rowdy, high-spirited bunch, and she was young herself and full of fun. She really contributed a lot toward the shaping of the Jackson 5, and I'll never be able to thank her enough for all she did.

I remember Suzanne showing us these charcoal sketches of the five of us. In each sketch we had a different hairstyle. In another set of color drawings we were all pictured in different clothes that could be switched around like Colorforms. After we all decided on the hairstyles, they took us to a barber so he could make us match up with our pictures. Then, after she showed us the clothes, we went down to a wardrobe department where they gave us outfits to try on. They'd see us in one set of clothes, decide the clothes weren't right, and we'd all go back to the Colorforms to "try on" some more.

We had classes in manners and grammar. They gave us a list of questions, and they said they were the kinds of questions that we could expect people to ask us. We were always being asked about our interests and our hometown and how we liked singing together. Fans and reporters alike wanted to know how old we each were when we started performing. It was hard to have your life turn into public property, even if you appreciated that people were interested in you because of your music.

The Motown people tested us on the answers to questions we hadn't heard from anyone yet. They tested us on grammar. And table manners. When we were ready, they brought us in for the last alterations on our sleeves and the trimming of our new Afros.

After all that there was a new song to learn called "I Want You Back." The song had a story behind it that we found out about little by little. It was written by someone from Chicago named Freddie Perren. He had been Jerry Butler's pianist when we opened for Jerry in a Chicago nightclub. He had felt sorry for these little kids the club owner had hired, figuring the club couldn't afford to get anyone else. His opinion changed dramatically when he saw us perform.

As it turned out, "I Want You Back" was originally called "I Want to Be Free" and was written for Gladys Knight. Freddie had even thought that Berry might go over Gladys's head and give the song to the Supremes. Instead, he mentioned to Jerry that he'd just signed this group of kids from Gary, Indiana. Freddie put two and two together, realized it was us, and decided to trust fate.

When we were learning the Steeltown songs back in Gary, Tito and Jermaine had to pay special attention because they were responsible for playing on those records. When they heard the demo for "I Want You Back," they listened to the guitar and bass parts, but Dad explained that Motown didn't expect them to play on our records; the rhythm track would be taken care of before we put our vocals down. But he reminded them that this would put more pressure on them to keep up their practice independently, because we'd have to duplicate those songs in front of our fans. In the meantime, all of us had lyrics and cues to learn.

The guys looking after us in the singing department were Freddy Perrin and Bobby Taylor and Deke Richards, who, along with Hal Davis and another Motown guy named "Fonce" Mizell, were part of the team that wrote and produced our first singles. Together these guys were called "The Corporation." We went over to Richards's apartment to rehearse, and he was impressed that we had prepared so well. He didn't have to do much tinkering with the vocal arrangement he'd worked out, and he thought that while we were still hot, we should go right to the studio and cut our parts. The following afternoon we went to the studio. We were all so happy with what we got that we took our rough mix over to Berry Gordy. It was still midafternoon when we arrived at his studio. We figured that once Berry heard it, we'd be home in time for supper.

But it was one in the morning when I finally slumped

in the back seat of Richards's car, bobbing and steadying my head all the way home to fight off sleep. Gordy hadn't liked the song we did. We went over every part again, and when we did, Gordy figured out what changes he had to make in the arrangement. He was trying new things with us, like a school chorus master who has everyone singing their part as if they're singing alone, even if you can't hear him or her distinctly for the crowd. After he was through rehearsing us as a group, and he had reworked the music, he took me aside, one on one, to explain my part. He told me exactly what he wanted and how he wanted me to help him get it. Then he explained everything to Freddie Perren, who was going to record it. Berry was brilliant in this area. Right after the single was released, we went in to cut an album. We were particularly impressed with the "I Want You Back" session then because that one song took more time (and tape) than all the other songs on the record combined. That's the way Motown did things in those days because Berry insisted on perfection and attention to detail. I'll never forget his persistence. This was his genius. Then and later, I observed every moment of the sessions where Berry was present and never forgot what I learned. To this day I use the same principles. Berry was my teacher and a great one. He could identify the little elements that would make a song *great* rather than just good. It was like magic, as if Berry was sprinkling pixie dust over everything.

For me and my brothers, recording for Motown was an exciting experience. Our team of writers shaped our music by being with us as we recorded it over and over, molding and sculpting a song until it was just perfect. We would cut a track over and over for *weeks* until we got it just as they wanted it. And I could see while they were doing it that it was getting better and better. They would change words, arrangements, rhythms, everything. Berry gave them the freedom to work this way because of his own perfectionist nature. I guess if they hadn't been doing it, he would have. Berry had such a knack. He'd just walk into the room where we were working and tell me what to do and he'd be right. It was amazing.

When "I Want You Back" was released in November 1969, it sold two million copies in six weeks and went to number one. Our next single, "ABC," came out in March 1970 and sold two million records in three weeks. I still like the part where I say, "Siddown, girl! I think I loove you! No, get up, girl, *show me what you can do!*" When our third single, "The Love You Save," went to number one in June of 1970, Berry's promise came true.

When our next single, "I'll Be There," was also a big hit in the fall of that year, we realized we might even surpass Berry's expectations and be able to pay him back for all the effort he had made for us.

My brothers and I—our whole family—were very proud. We had created a new sound for a new decade. It was the first time in recording history that a bunch of kids had made so many hit records. The Jackson 5 had never had much competition from kids our own age. In the amateur days there was a kids' group called the Five Stairsteps that we used to see. They were good, but they didn't seem to have the strong family unit that we did, and sadly they broke up. After "ABC" hit the charts in such a big way, we started seeing other groups that record companies were grooming to ride the bandwagon we had built. I enjoyed all these groups: the Partridge Family, the Osmonds, the DeFranco Family. The Osmonds were already around, but they were doing a much different style of music, like barbershop harmony and crooning. As soon as we hit, they and the other groups got into soul real fast. We didn't mind. Competition, as we knew, was healthy. Our own relatives thought "One Bad Apple" was us. I remember being so little that they had a special apple crate for me to stand on with my name on it so I could reach the microphone. Microphones didn't go down far enough for kids my age. So many of my childhood years went by that way, with me standing on that apple box singing my heart out while other kids were outside playing.

As I said before, in those early days "The Corporation" at Motown produced and shaped all our music. I remember lots of times when I felt the song should be sung one way and the producers felt it should be sung another way. But for a long time I was very obedient and wouldn't say anything about it. Finally it reached a point where I got fed up with being told exactly how to sing. This was in 1972 when I was fourteen years old, around the time of the song "Lookin' Through the Windows." They wanted me to sing a certain way, and I knew they were wrong. No matter what age you are, if you *have* it and you *know* it, then people should listen to you. I was furious with our producers and very upset. So I called Berry Gordy and complained. I said that they had always told me how to sing, and I had agreed all this time, but now they were getting too . . . mechanical.

So he came into the studio and told them to let me do what I wanted to do. I think he told them to let me be more free or something. And after that, I started adding a lot of vocal twists that they really ended up loving. I'd do a lot of ad-libbing, like twisting words or adding some edge to them.

When Berry was in the studio with us, he would always add something that was right. He'd go from studio to studio, checking on different aspects of people's work, often adding elements that made the records better. Walt Disney used to do the same thing; he'd go check on his various artists and say, "Well, this character should be more outgoing." I always knew when Berry was enjoying something I was doing in the studio, because he has this habit of rolling his tongue in his cheek when he's pleased by something. If things were really going well, he'd punch the air like the ex-professional boxer he is.

My three favorite songs from those days are "Never Can Say Goodbye," "I'll Be There," and "ABC." I'll never forget the first time I heard "ABC." I thought it was *so* good. I remember feeling this eagerness to sing that song, to get in the studio and really make it *work* for us.

We were still rehearsing daily and working hard—some things didn't change—but we were grateful to be where we were. There were so many people pulling for us, and we were so determined ourselves that it seemed anything could happen.

Once "I Want You Back" came out, everyone at Motown prepared us for success. Diana loved it and presented us at a big-name Hollywood discotheque, where she had us playing in a comfortable party atmosphere like at Berry's. Following directly on the heels of Diana's event came an invitation to play at the "Miss Black America" telecast. Being on the show would enable us to give people a preview of our record *and* our show. After we got the invitation, my brothers and I remembered our disappointment at not getting to go to New York to do our first TV show because Motown had called. Now we were going to do our first TV show *and* we were with Motown. Life was very good. Diana, of course, put the cherry on top. She was going to host "The Hollywood Palace," a big Saturday night show; it would be her last appearance with the Supremes and the first major exposure for us. This meant a lot to Motown, because by then they had decided that our new album would be called "Diana Ross Presents the Jackson 5." Never before had a superstar like Diana passed the torch to a bunch of kids. Motown, Diana, and five kids from Gary, Indiana, were all pretty excited. By then "I Want You Back" had come out, and Berry was proven right again; all the stations that played Sly and the Beatles were playing us, too.

As I mentioned earlier, we didn't work as hard on the album as we did on the single, but we had fun trying out all sorts of songs—from "Who's Lovin' You," the old Miracles' song we were doing in the talent show days, to "Zip-A-Dee-Doo-Dah."

We did songs on that album that appealed to a wide

audience—kids, teenagers, and grownups—and we all felt
that was a reason for its big success. We knew that "The
Hollywood Palace" had a live audience, a sophisticated
Hollywood crowd, and we were concerned; but we had
them from the first note. There was an orchestra in the
pit, so that was the first time I heard *all* of "I Want You
Back" performed live because I wasn't there when they
recorded the strings for the album. Doing that show made
us feel like kings, the way winning the citywide show in
Gary had.

Selecting the right songs for us to do was going to be a
real challenge now that we weren't depending on other
people's hits to win a crowd. The Corporation guys and
Hal Davis were put to work writing songs especially for
us, as well as producing them. Berry didn't want to have
to bail us all out again. So even after our first singles hit
number one on the charts, we were busy with the follow-
ups.

"I Want You Back" could have been sung by a grown-
up, but "ABC" and "The Love You Save" were written for
our young voices, with parts for Jermaine as well as me—
another bow to the Sly sound, which rotated singers
around the stage. The Corporation had also written those
songs with dance routines in mind: the steps our fans did
at parties as well as those we did on stage. The verses were

tongue-twisting, and that's why they were split up between Jermaine and me.

Neither of those records could have happened without "I Want You Back." We were adding and subtracting
ideas in the arrangements from that one mother lode of a
song, but the public seemed to want everything we were
doing. We later made two more records in the vein,
"Mama's Pearl" and "Sugar Daddy," which reminded me
of my own schoolyard days: "While I'm giving you the
candy, *he's* getting all your love!" We added one new
wrinkle when Jermaine and I sang harmony together,
which always got an enthusiastic response when we did it
from the same mike on stage.

The pros have told us that no group had a better start
than we did. Ever.

"I'll Be There" was our real breakthrough song; it was the
one that said, "We're here to stay." It was number one for
five weeks, which is *very* unusual. That's a long time for a
song and the song was one of my favorites of all the songs
we've ever done. How I loved the words: "You and I must
make a pact, we must bring salvation back . . ." Willie
Hutch and Berry Gordy didn't seem like people who'd
write like that. They were always kidding around with us
when we weren't in the studio. But that song grabbed me

from the moment I heard the demo. I didn't even know what a harpsichord was until that record's opening notes were played for us. The song was produced thanks to the genius of Hal Davis, assisted by Suzy Ikeda, my other half who stood next to me song after song, making sure I put the right emotion and feeling and heart into the composition. It was a serious song, but we threw in a fun part when I sang "Just look over your shoulder, honey!" Without the honey, that's right out of the Four Tops' great song "Reach Out, I'll Be There." So we were feeling more and more like a part of Motown's history as well as its future.

Originally the plan was for me to sing all the bouncy stuff and Jermaine to do the ballads. But though Jermaine's voice at seventeen was more mature, ballads were more my love, if not really my style—yet. That was our fourth straight number one as a group, and a lot of people liked Jermaine's song "I Found That Girl," the B-side of "The Love You Save," just as much as the hits.

We worked those songs into one big medley, with plenty of room for dancing, and we went back to that medley when we performed on all kinds of TV shows. For instance, we played on "The Ed Sullivan Show" three different times. Motown always told us what to say in interviews back then, but Mr. Sullivan was one of the people who drew us out and made us feel comfortable.

Looking back, I wouldn't say Motown was putting us in any kind of straitjacket or turning us into robots, even though I wouldn't have done it that way myself; and if I had children, I wouldn't tell them what to say. The Motown people were doing something with us that hadn't been done before, and who was to say what was the right way to handle that sort of stuff?

Reporters would ask us all kinds of questions, and the Motown people would be standing by to help us out or monitor the questions if need be. We wouldn't have dreamed of trying anything that would embarrass them. I guess they were worried about the possibility of our sounding militant the way people were often doing in those days. Maybe they were worried after they gave us those Afros that they had created little Frankensteins. Once a reporter asked a Black Power question and the Motown person told him we didn't think about that stuff because we were a "commercial product." It sounded weird, but we winked and gave the power salute when we left, which seemed to thrill the guy.

We even had a reunion with Don Cornelius on his "Soul Train" show. He had been a local disc jockey during our Chicago days, so we all knew one another from that time. We enjoyed watching his show and picked up ideas from those dancers who were from our part of the country.

The crazy days of the big Jackson 5 tours began right after the successes we had with our records. It started with a big arena tour in the fall of 1970; we played huge halls like Madison Square Garden and the Los Angeles Forum. When "Never Can Say Goodbye" was a big hit in 1971, we played forty-five cities that summer, followed by fifty more cities later that year.

I recall most of that time as a period of extreme closeness with my brothers. We have always been a very loyal and affectionate group. We clowned around, goofed off a lot together, and played outrageous pranks on each other and the people who worked with us. We never got too rowdy—no TVs sailed out of our hotel windows, but a lot of water was spilled on various heads. We were mostly trying to conquer the boredom we felt from being so long on the road. When you're bored on tour, you tend to do anything to cheer yourself up. Here we were, cramped up in these hotel rooms, unable to go anywhere because of the mobs of screaming girls outside, and we wanted to have some fun. I wish we could have captured some of the stuff we did on film, especially some of the wild pranks. We'd all wait until our security manager, Bill Bray, was asleep. Then we'd stage insane fast-walk races in the hallways, pillow fights, tag-team wrestling matches, shaving cream wars, you name it. We were nuts. We'd drop balloons and paper bags full of water off hotel balconies and watch them explode. Then we'd die laughing. We threw stuff at each other and spent hours on the phone making fake calls and ordering immense room service meals that were delivered to the rooms of strangers. Anyone who walked into one of our bedrooms had a ninety percent chance of being drenched by a bucket of water propped over the doors.

When we'd arrive in a new city, we'd try to do all the sightseeing we could. We traveled with a wonderful tutor, Rose Fine, who taught us a great deal and made sure we did our lessons. It was Rose who instilled in me a love of books and literature that sustains me today. I read everything I could get my hands on. New cities meant new places to shop. We loved to shop, especially in bookstores and department stores, but as our fame spread our fans transformed casual shopping trips into hand-to-hand combat. Being mobbed by near hysterical girls was one of the most terrifying experiences for me in those days. I mean, it was *rough.* We'd decide to run into some department store to see what they had, and the fans would find out we were there and would demolish the place, just tear it up.

Counters would get knocked over, glass would break, the cash registers would be toppled. All we had wanted to do was look at some clothes! When those mob scenes broke out, all the craziness and adulation and notoriety became more than we could handle. If you haven't witnessed a scene like that, you can't imagine what it's like. Those girls were *serious*. They still are. They don't realize they might hurt you because they're acting out of love. They mean well, but I can testify that it *hurts* to be mobbed. You feel as if you're going to suffocate or be dismembered. There are a thousand hands grabbing at you. One girl is twisting your wrist this way while another girl is pulling your watch off. They grab your hair and pull it hard, and it hurts like fire. You fall against things and the scrapes are horrible. I still wear the scars, and I can remember in which city I got each of them. Early on, I learned how to run through crowds of thrashing girls outside of theaters, hotels, and airports. It's important to remember to shield your eyes with your hands because girls can forget they have nails during such emotional confrontations. I know the fans mean well and I love them for their enthusiasm and support, but crowd scenes *are* scary.

The wildest mob scene I ever witnessed happened the first time we went to England. We were in the air over the Atlantic when the pilot announced that he had just been told there were ten thousand kids waiting for us at Heathrow Airport. We couldn't believe it. We were excited, but if we could have turned around and flown home, we might have. We knew this was going to be something, but since there wasn't enough fuel to go back, we flew on. When we landed, we could see that the fans had literally taken over the whole airport. It was wild to be mobbed like that. My brothers and I felt fortunate to make it out of the airport alive that day.

I wouldn't trade my memories of those days with my brothers for anything. I often wish I could relive those days. We were like the seven dwarfs: each of us was different, each had his own personality. Jackie was the athlete and the worrier. Tito was the strong, compassionate father figure. He was totally into cars and loved putting them together and tearing them apart. Jermaine was the one I was closest to when we were growing up. He was funny and easygoing, and was constantly fooling around. It was Jermaine who put all those buckets of cold water on the doors of our hotel rooms. Marlon was and is one of the most determined people I've ever met. He, too, was a real joker and prankster. He used to be the one who'd always get in trouble in the early days because he'd be out of step or miss a note, but that was far from true later.

The diversity of my brothers' personalities and the closeness we felt were what kept me going during those gruelling days of constant touring. Everybody helped everybody. Jackie and Tito would keep us from going too far with our pranks. They'd seem to have us under control, and then Jermaine and Marlon would shout, "Let's go crazy!!"

I really miss all that. In the early days we were together all the time. We'd go to amusement parks or ride horses or watch movies. We did everything together. As soon as someone said, "I'm going swimming," we'd all yell, "Me too!"

The separation from my brothers started much later, when they began to get married. An understandable change occurred as each of them became closest to his wife and *they* became a family unit unto themselves. A part of me wanted us to stay as we were—brothers who were also best friends—but change is inevitable and always good in one sense or another. We still love each other's company. We still have a great time when we're together. But the various paths our lives have taken won't allow us the freedom to enjoy one another's company as much as we did.

In those days, touring with the Jackson 5, I always shared a room with Jermaine. He and I were close, both onstage and off, and shared a lot of the same interests. Since Jermaine was also the brother most intrigued by the girls who wanted to get at him, he and I would get into mischief on the road.

I think our father decided early on that he had to keep a more watchful eye on us than on our other brothers. He would usually take the room next to ours, which meant he could come in to check on us anytime through the connecting doors. I really despised this arrangement, not only because he could monitor our misbehavior, but also because he used to do the meanest things to us. Jermaine and I would be sleeping, exhausted after a show, and my father would bring a bunch of girls into the room; we'd wake up and they'd be standing there, looking at us, giggling.

Because show business and my career were my life, the biggest personal struggle I had to face during those teenage years did not involve the recording studios or my stage performance. In those days, the biggest struggle was right there in my mirror. To a great degree, my identity as a person was tied to my identity as a celebrity.

My appearance began to really change when I was about fourteen. I grew quite a bit in height. People who didn't know me would come into a room expecting to be introduced to cute little Michael Jackson and they'd walk right past me. I would say, "I'm Michael," and they would look doubtful. Michael was a cute little kid; I was a gangly adolescent heading toward five feet ten inches. I was not the person they expected or even wanted to see. Adolescence is hard enough, but imagine having your own natural insecurities about the changes your body is undergoing heightened by the negative reactions of others. They seemed so surprised that I could change, that my body was undergoing the same natural change everyone's does.

It was tough. Everyone had called me cute for a long time, but along with all the other changes, my skin broke out in a terrible case of acne. I looked in the mirror one morning and it was like, "OH NO!" I seemed to have a pimple for every oil gland. And the more I was bothered by it, the worse it got. I didn't realize it then, but my diet of greasy processed food didn't help either.

I became subconsciously scarred by this experience with my skin. I got very shy and became embarrassed to meet people because my complexion was so bad. It really seemed that the more I looked in the mirror, the worse the pimples got. My appearance began to depress me. So I know that a case of acne can have a devastating effect on a person. The effect on me was so bad that it messed up my whole personality. I couldn't look at people when I talked to them. I'd look down, or away. I felt I didn't have anything to be proud of and I didn't even want to go out. I didn't do anything.

My brother Marlon would be covered with pimples and he wouldn't care but I didn't want to see anybody and I didn't want anyone to see my skin in that shape. It makes you wonder about what makes us the way we are, that two brothers could be so different.

I still had our hit records to be proud of, and once I hit the stage, I didn't think about anything else. All that worry was gone.

But once I came offstage, there was that mirror to face again.

Eventually, things changed. I started feeling differently about my condition. I've learned to change how I think and learned to feel better about myself. Most important, I changed my diet. That was the key.

In the fall of 1971 I cut my first solo record, "Got to Be There." It was wonderful working on that record and it became one of my favorites. It was Berry Gordy's idea that I should do a solo recording, and so I became one of the first people in a Motown group to really step out. Berry also said he thought I should record my own album. Years later, when I did, I realized he was right.

There was a small conflict during that era that was typical of the struggles I went through as a young singer.

When you're young and have ideas, people often think you're just being childish and silly. We were on tour in 1972, the year "Got to Be There" became a big hit. One night I said to our road manager, "Before I sing that song, let me go offstage and grab that little hat I wore for the picture on the album cover. If the audience sees me wearing that hat, they'll go crazy."

He thought it was the most ridiculous idea he had ever heard. I was not allowed to do it because I was young, and *they* all thought it was a dumb idea. Not long after that incident, Donny Osmond began wearing a very similar hat all over the country and people *loved* it. I felt good about my instincts; I had thought it would work. I had seen Marvin Gaye wear a hat when he sang "Let's Get It On," and people went bananas. They knew what was coming when Marvin put that hat on. It added excitement and communicated something to the audience that allowed them to become more involved with the show.

I was already a devoted fan of film and animation by the time "The Jackson Five" Saturday morning cartoon show started appearing over network television in 1971. Diana Ross had enhanced my appreciation of animation when she taught me to draw, but being a cartoon character pushed me over the brink into a full-time love of the movies and the kind of animated motion pictures pioneered by Walt Disney. I have such admiration for Mr. Disney and what he accomplished with the help of so many talented artists. When I think about the joy he and his company have brought to millions of children—and adults—the world over, I am in awe.

I loved being a cartoon. It was so much fun to get up on Saturday mornings to watch cartoons and look forward to seeing ourselves on the screen. It was like a fantasy come true for all of us.

My first real involvement with films came when I sang the title song for the movie *Ben* in 1972.

Ben meant a lot to me. Nothing had ever excited me as much as going to the studio to put my voice on film. I had a great time. Later, when the movie came out, I'd go to the theater and wait until the end when the credits would flash on, and it would say, " 'Ben' sung by Michael Jackson." I was really impressed by that. I loved the song and loved the story. Actually, the story was a lot like *E.T.* It was about a boy who befriended a rat. People didn't understand the boy's love for this little creature. He was dying of some disease and his only true friend was Ben, the leader of the rats in the city where they lived. A lot of people thought the movie was a bit odd, but I was not one of them. The song went to number one and is still a favorite of mine. I have always loved animals and I enjoy reading about them and seeing movies in which they're featured.

CHAPTER
THREE

DANCING MACHINE

The media write weird stuff about me all the time. The distortion of the truth bothers me. I usually don't read a lot of what is printed, although I often hear about it.

I don't understand why they feel the need to make up things about me. I suppose if there's nothing scandalous to report, it's necessary to make things interesting. I take some small pride in thinking that I've come out pretty well, all things considered. A lot of children in the entertainment business ended up doing drugs and destroying themselves: Frankie Lymon, Bobbie Driscoll, any of a number of child stars. And I can understand their turning to drugs, considering the enormous stresses put upon them at a young age. It's a difficult life. Very few manage to maintain any semblance of a normal childhood.

I myself have never even tried drugs—no marijuana, no cocaine, nothing. I mean, I haven't even *tried* these things.

Forget it.

This isn't to say we were never tempted. We were musicians doing business during an era when drug use was common. I don't mean to be judgmental—it's not even a moral issue for me—but I've seen drugs destroy too many lives to think they're anything to fool with. I'm certainly no angel, and I may have my own bad habits, but drugs aren't among them.

By the time *Ben* came out, we knew that we were going to go around the world. American soul music had become as popular in other countries as blue jeans and hamburgers. We were invited to become a part of that big world, and in 1972 we began our first overseas tour with a visit to England. Though we'd never been there before or appeared on British television, people knew all the words to our songs. They even had wide scarves with our pictures on them and "Jackson 5" written in big broad letters. The theaters were smaller than the ones we were used to playing in the United States, but the enthusiasm from the

crowds was very gratifying as we'd finish each song. They
didn't scream *during* the songs the way crowds did back
home, so people over there could actually tell how good
Tito was getting on the guitar, because they could hear
him.

We took Randy along because we wanted to give him
the experience and allow him to see what was going on.
He wasn't officially part of our act, but stayed in the background with bongos. He had his own Jackson 5 outfit, so
when we introduced him, people cheered. The next time
we came back, Randy would be a part of the group. I had
been the bongo player before Randy, and Marlon had
played them before me, so it had become almost a tradition to break the new guy in on those crazy little drums.

We had three years of hits behind us when we toured
Europe that first time, so there was enough to please both
the kids who followed our music and the Queen of England, whom we met at a Royal Command Performance.
That was very exciting for us. I had seen photographs of
other groups, like the Beatles, meeting the Queen after
command performances, but I never dreamed we'd get
the chance to play for her.

England was our jumping-off point, and it was different from any place we'd been before, but the farther we
traveled, the more exotic the world looked. We saw the

great museums of Paris and the beautiful mountains of Switzerland. Europe was an education in the roots of Western culture and, in a way, a preparation for visiting Eastern countries that were more spiritual. I was very impressed that the people there didn't value material things as much as they did animals and nature. For instance, China and Japan were places that helped me grow because these countries made me understand there was more to life than the things you could hold in your hand or see with your eyes. And in all of these countries, the people had heard of us and liked our music.

Australia and New Zealand, our next stops, were English-speaking, but we met people who were still living in tribes in the outback. They greeted us as brothers even though they didn't speak our language. If I'd ever needed proof that all men could be brothers, I certainly had it during that tour.

And then there was Africa. We had read up on Africa because our tutor, Miss Fine, had prepared special lessons on the customs and history of each country we visited. We didn't get to see the prettier parts of Africa, but the ocean and the shore and the people were unbelievably beautiful near the coast where we were. We went to a game reserve one day and observed animals roaming wild. The music was eye-opening too. The rhythms were phenomenal.

When we first came off the plane, it was dawn and there was a long line of Africans dancing in their native costumes, with drums and shakers. They were dancing all around, welcoming us. They were really into it. Boy, it was something. What a perfect way to welcome us to Africa. I'll never forget that.

And the craftspeople in the marketplace were incredible. People were making things as we watched and selling other things. I remember one man who made beautiful wood carvings. He'd ask you what you wanted and you'd say, "A man's face," and he'd take a piece from a tree trunk, slice it, and create this remarkable face. You could watch him do it right before your eyes. I'd just sit there and watch people step up to ask him to make something for them and he'd do this whole thing over and over.

It was a visit to Senegal that made us realize how fortunate we were and how our African heritage had helped to make us what we were. We visited an old, abandoned slave camp at Gore Island and we were so moved. The African people had given us gifts of courage and endurance that we couldn't hope to repay.

I guess if Motown could have had us age the way they wanted us to, they would have wanted Jackie to stay the age he was when we became a headline act and have each of us catch up with him—although I think they'd have wanted to keep me a year or so younger, so I could still be a child star. That may sound nonsensical, but it really wasn't much more farfetched than the way they were continuing to mold us, keeping us from being a real group with its own internal direction and ideas. We were growing up and we were expanding creatively. We had so many ideas we wanted to try out, but they were convinced that we shouldn't fool with a successful formula. At least they didn't drop us as soon as my voice changed, as some said they might.

It got to the point that it seemed there were more guys in the booth than there were on the studio floor at any given time. They all seemed to be bumping into one another, giving advice and monitoring our music.

Our loyal fans stuck with us on records like "I Am Love" and "Skywriter." These songs were musically ambitious pop recordings, with sophisticated string arrangements, but they weren't right for us. Sure, we couldn't do "ABC" all our lives—that was the last thing we wanted—but even the older fans thought "ABC" had more going for it, and that was hard for us to live with. During the mid-seventies we were in danger of becoming an oldies act, and I wasn't even eighteen yet.

When Jermaine married Hazel Gordy, our boss's

daughter, people were winking at us, saying that we'd always be looked after. Indeed, when "Get It Together" came out in 1973, it got the same treatment from Berry that "I Want You Back" had gotten. It was our biggest hit in two years, though you could have said it was more like a bone transplant than the spanking little baby that our first hit was. Nevertheless, "Get It Together" had good, tough low harmony, a sharper wah-wah guitar, and strings that buzzed like fireflies. Radio stations liked it, but not as much as the new dance clubs called discos did. Motown picked up on this and brought back Hal Davis from The Corporation days to really put the juice into "Dancing Machine." The Jackson 5 were no longer just the backup group for the 101 Strings or whatever.

Motown had come a long way from the early days when you could find good studio musicians supplementing their session pay with bowling alley gigs. A new sophistication turned up in the music on "Dancing Machine." That song had the best horn part we'd worked with yet and a "bubble machine" in the break, made out of synthesizer noise, that kept the song from going completely out of style. Disco music had its detractors, but to us it seemed our rite of passage into the adult world.

I loved "Dancing Machine," loved the groove and the feel of that song. When it came out in 1974, I was determined to find a dance move that would enhance the song and make it more exciting to perform—and, I hoped, more exciting to watch.

So when we sang "Dancing Machine" on "Soul Train," I did a street-style dance move called the Robot. That performance was a lesson to me in the power of television. Overnight, "Dancing Machine" rose to the top of the charts, and within a few days it seemed that every kid in the United States was doing the Robot. I had never seen anything like it.

Motown and the Jackson 5 could agree on one thing: As our act grew, our audience should too. We had two re-cruits coming up: Randy had already toured with us, and Janet was showing talent with her singing and dancing lessons. We couldn't put Randy and Janet into our old lineup any more than we could put square pegs into round holes. I wouldn't insult their considerable talent by saying that show business was so in their blood that they just took their places automatically, as if we'd reserved a spot for them. They worked hard and earned their places in the group. They didn't join us because they ate meals with us and shared our old toys.

If you just went by blood, I'd have as much crane operator in me as singer. You can't measure these things.

Dad worked us hard and kept certain goals in sight while spinning dreams at night.

Just as disco might have seemed like a very unlikely place for a kids' group to become a grown-up act, Las Vegas, with its showcase theaters, wasn't exactly the family atmosphere that Motown had originally groomed us for, but we decided to play there just the same. There wasn't much to do in Las Vegas if you didn't gamble, but we thought of the theaters in the city as just big clubs with the club hours and clientele of our Gary and South Side Chicago days—except for the tourists. Tourist crowds were a good thing for us, since they knew our old hits and would watch our skits and listen to new songs without getting restless. It was great to see the delight on their faces when little Janet came out in her Mae West costume for a number or two.

We had performed skits before, in a 1971 TV special called *Goin' Back to Indiana,* which celebrated our Gary homecoming the first time we all decided to return. Our records had become hits all over the world since we'd seen our hometown last.

It was even more fun to do skits with nine of us, instead of just five, plus whatever guests happened to appear with us. Our expanded lineup was a dream come true for Dad. Looking back, I know the Las Vegas shows were an experience I'll never recapture. We didn't have the high-pressure concert crowd wanting all our hit songs and nothing more. We were temporarily freed from the pressures of having to keep up with what everyone else was doing. We had a ballad or two in every show to break in my "new voice." At fifteen, I was having to think about things like that.

There were people from CBS Television at our Las Vegas shows and they approached us about doing a variety show for the upcoming summer. We were very interested and pleased that we were being recognized as more than just a "Motown group." Over time, this distinction would not be lost on us. Because we had creative control over our Las Vegas revue, it was harder for us to return to our lack of freedom in recording and writing music once we got back to Los Angeles. We'd always intended to grow and develop in the musical field. That was our bread and butter, and we felt we were being held back. Sometimes I felt we were being treated as if we still lived in Berry Gordy's house—and with Jermaine now a son-in-law, our frustration was only heightened.

By the time we began putting our own act together, there were signs that other Motown institutions were changing. Marvin Gaye took charge of his own music and produced his masterpiece album, *What's Goin' On.*

Stevie Wonder was learning more about electronic keyboards than the experienced studio hired guns—they were coming to him for advice. One of our last great memories from our Motown days is of Stevie leading us in chanting to back up his tough, controversial song "You Haven't Done Nothin'." Though Stevie and Marvin were still in the Motown camp, they had fought for—and won—the right to make their own records, and even to publish their own songs. Motown hadn't even budged with us. To them we were still kids, even if they weren't dressing us and "protecting" us any longer.

Our problems with Motown began around 1974, when we told them in no uncertain terms that we wanted to write and produce our own songs. Basically, we didn't like the way our music sounded at the time. We had a strong competitive urge and we felt we were in danger of being eclipsed by other groups who were creating a more contemporary sound.

Motown said, "No, you can't write your own songs; you've got to have songwriters and producers." They not only refused to grant our requests, they told us it was taboo to even mention that we wanted to do our own music. I really got discouraged and began to seriously dislike all the material Motown was feeding us. Eventually I became so disappointed and upset that I wanted to leave Motown behind.

When I feel that something is not right, I have to speak up. I know most people don't think of me as tough or strong-willed, but that's just because they don't know me. Eventually my brothers and I reached a point with Motown where we were miserable but no one was saying anything. My brothers didn't say anything. My father didn't say anything. So it was up to me to arrange a meeting with Berry Gordy and talk to him. I was the one who had to say that we—the Jackson 5—were going to leave Motown. I went over to see him, face to face, and it was one of the most difficult things I've ever done. If I had been the only one of us who was unhappy, I might have kept my mouth shut, but there had been so much talk at home about how unhappy we *all* were that I went in and talked to him and told him how we felt. I told him I was unhappy.

Remember, I love Berry Gordy. I think he's a genius, a brilliant man who's one of the giants of the music business. I have nothing but respect for him, but that day I was a lion. I complained that we weren't allowed any freedom to write songs and produce. He told me that he still thought we needed outside producers to make hit records.

But I knew better. Berry was talking out of anger. That was a difficult meeting, but we're friends again, and he's still like a father to me—very proud of me and happy about my success. No matter what, I will always love Berry because he taught me some of the most valuable things I've learned in my life. He's the man who told the Jackson 5 they would become a part of history, and that is exactly what happened. Motown has done so much for so many people over the years. I feel we're fortunate to have been one of the groups Berry personally introduced to the public and I owe enormous thanks to this man. My life would have been very different without him. We all felt that Motown started us, supporting our professional careers. We all felt our roots were there, and we all wished we could stay. We were grateful for everything they had done for us, but change is inevitable. I'm a person of the present, and I have to ask, How are things going now? What's happening now? What's going to happen in the future that could affect what has happened in the past?

It's important for artists always to maintain control of their lives and work. There's been a big problem in the past with artists being taken advantage of. I've learned that a person *can* prevent that from happening by standing up for what he or she believes is right, without concern for the consequences. We could have stayed with Motown; but if we had, we'd probably be an oldies act.

I knew it was time for change, so we followed our instincts, and we won when we decided to try for a fresh start with another label, Epic.

We were relieved that we had finally made our feelings clear and cut the ties that were binding us, but we were also really devastated when Jermaine decided to stay with Motown. He was Berry's son-in-law and his situation was more complicated than ours. He thought it was more important for him to stay than to leave, and Jermaine always did as his conscience told him, so he left the group.

I clearly remember the first show we did without him, because it was so painful for me. Since my earliest days on the stage—and even in our rehearsals in our Gary living room—Jermaine stood at my left with his bass. I *depended* on being next to Jermaine. And when I did that first show without him there, with no one next to me, I felt totally naked onstage for the first time in my life. So we worked harder to compensate for the loss of one of our shining stars, Jermaine. I remember that show well because we got three standing ovations. We worked *hard*.

When Jermaine left the group, Marlon had a chance to take his place and he really shone onstage. My brother

Randy officially took my place as bongo player and the baby of the band.

Around the time that Jermaine left, things were further complicated for us because of the fact that we were doing a stupid summer replacement TV series. It was a dumb move to agree to do that show and I hated every minute of it.

I had loved the old "Jackson Five" cartoon show. I used to wake up early on Saturday mornings and say, "I'm a cartoon!" But I hated doing this television show because I felt it would hurt our recording career rather than help it. I think a TV series is the worst thing an artist who has a recording career can do. I kept saying, "But this is gonna hurt our record sales." And others said, "No, it's gonna help them."

They were totally wrong. We had to dress in ridiculous outfits and perform stupid comedy routines to canned laughter. It was all so fake. We didn't have time to learn or master anything about television. We had to create three dance numbers a day, trying to meet a deadline. The Nielsen ratings controlled our lives from week to week. I'd never do it again. It's a dead-end road. What happens is partly psychological. You are in people's homes every week and they begin to feel they know you too well. You're doing all this silly comedy to canned laughter and your music begins to recede into the background. When you try to get serious again and pick up your career where you left off, you can't because you're overexposed. People are thinking of you as the guys who do the silly, crazy routines. One week you're Santa Claus, the next week you're Prince Charming, another week you're a rabbit. It's crazy, because you lose your identity in the business; the rocker image you had is gone. I'm not a comedian. I'm not a show host. I'm a musician. That's why I've turned down offers to host the Grammy Awards and the American Music Awards. Is it really entertaining for me to get up there and crack a few weak jokes and force people to laugh because I'm Michael Jackson, when I know in my heart that I'm not funny?

After our TV show I can remember doing theaters-in-the-round where the stage didn't revolve because if they had turned it, we would have been singing to some empty seats. I learned something from that experience and I was the one who refused to renew our contract with the network for another season. I just told my father and brothers that I thought it was a big mistake, and they understood my point of view. I had actually had a lot of misgivings about the show *before* we started taping it, but I ended up agreeing to give it a try because everyone thought it would be a great experience and very good for us.

The problem with TV is that everything must be crammed into a little space of time. You don't have time to perfect anything. Schedules—tight schedules—rule your life. If you're not happy with something, you just forget it and move on to the next routine. I'm a perfectionist by nature. I like things to be the best they can be. I want people to hear or watch something I've done and feel that I've given it everything I've got. I feel I owe an audience that courtesy. On the show our sets were sloppy, the lighting was often poor, and our choreography was *rushed*. Somehow, the show was a big hit. There was a popular show on opposite us and we beat them out in the Nielsens. CBS really wanted to keep us, but I knew that show was a mistake. As it turned out, it did hurt our record sales and it took us a while to recover from the damage. When you know something's wrong for you, you have to make difficult decisions and trust your instincts.

I rarely did TV after that; the *Motown 25* special is the only show that comes to mind. Berry asked me to be on that show and I kept trying to say no, but he finally talked me into it. I told him I wanted to do "Billie Jean" even though it would be the only non-Motown song on the show, and he readily agreed. "Billie Jean" was number one at the time. My brothers and I really rehearsed for the show. I choreographed our routines, so I was pretty wrapped up in those numbers, but I had a good notion of what I wanted to do with "Billie Jean." I had a sense that the routine had worked itself out in my mind while I was busy with other things. I asked someone to rent or buy me a black fedora—a spy hat—and the day of the show I began putting the routine together. I'll never forget that night, because when I opened my eyes at the end, people were on their feet applauding. I was overwhelmed by the reaction. It felt so good.

Our only "break" during the Motown-to-Epic switch was the TV show. While that was all going on, we heard that Epic had Kenny Gamble and Leon Huff working on demos for us. We were told we'd be recording in Philadelphia after our shows were all done.

If there was anyone who stood to gain the most from switching labels, it was Randy, who was now part of the Five. But now that he finally *was* one of us, we were no longer known as the Jackson 5. Motown said that the group's name was the company's registered trademark, and that we couldn't use it when we left. That was hardball, of course, so we called ourselves the Jacksons from that time on.

Dad had met with the Philly guys while negotiations were going on with Epic. We'd always had great respect for the records that Gamble and Huff had overseen, records like "Backstabbers" by the O'Jays, "If You Don't Know Me by Now," by Harold Melvin and the Blue Notes (featuring Teddy Pendergrass), and "When Will I See You Again," by the Three Degrees, along with many other hits. They told Dad they'd been watching us, and they said they wouldn't mess with our singing. Dad mentioned that we were hoping to have a song or two of our own included in the new album, and they promised to give them a fair hearing.

We'd gotten to talk with Kenny and Leon and their team of people, which included Leon McFadden and John Whitehead. They showed what they could do for themselves when they made "Ain't No Stoppin' Us Now" in 1979. Dexter Wanzel was also a part of this team. Kenny Gamble and Leon Huff are such pros. I actually got a chance to watch them create as they presented songs to us and that helped my songwriting a lot. Just watching Huff play the piano while Gamble sang taught me more about the anatomy of a song than anything else. Kenny Gamble is a master melody man. He made me pay closer attention to the melody because of watching him create. And I would watch, too. I'd sit there like a hawk, observing every decision, listening to every note. They'd come to us in our hotel and play a whole album's worth of music for us. That's the way we'd be introduced to the songs they had chosen for our album—aside from the two songs we were writing ourselves. It was an amazing thing to be present for.

We had cut some demos of our songs at home during our breaks from shooting, but we decided to wait on those —we felt there was no sense putting a gun to anyone's head. We knew that Philly had a lot to offer us, so we'd save our surprise for them later.

Our two songs, "Blues Away" and "Style of Life," were two hard secrets to keep at the time because we were so proud of them. "Style of Life" was a jam that Tito directed, and it was in keeping with the nightclub groove that "Dancing Machine" got us into, but we kept it a little leaner and meaner than Motown would have cut it.

"Blues Away" was one of my first songs, and though I don't sing it any more, I'm not embarrassed to hear it. I couldn't have gone on in this business if I had ended up hating my own records after all that work. It's a light song about overcoming a deep depression—I was going for the Jackie Wilson "Lonely Teardrops" way of laughing on the outside to stop the churning inside.

When we saw the cover art for *The Jacksons* album, the first we cut for Epic, we were surprised to see that we all looked alike. Even Tito looked skinny! I had my "crown"

Afro then, so I didn't stick out so much, I guess. Still, once we performed our new songs like "Enjoy Yourself" and "Show You the Way to Go," people knew I was still second from the left, right out front. Randy took Tito's old spot on my far right, and Tito moved into the old place Jermaine had. It took a long time for me to feel comfortable with that, as I've mentioned, though it was through no fault of Tito's.

Those two singles were fun records—"Enjoy Yourself" was great for dancing. It had rhythm guitar and horns that I really liked. It was also a number one record. For my taste, I leaned a little more toward "Show You the Way to Go" because it showed what good regard the Epic people had for our singing. We were all over that record and it was the best one we did. I loved the high hat and strings fluttering alongside us like birds' wings. I'm surprised that song in particular wasn't a bigger hit.

Though we couldn't spell it out, we kind of hinted about our situation in a song called "Living Together," which Kenny and Leon chose with us in mind. "If we're going to stick together, we've got to be a family. Have yourself a real good time, but don't you know it's getting late." The strings pointed and thrust like they did in "Backstabbers," but that was a Jacksons' message, even if it wasn't in the Jacksons' style—yet.

Gamble and Huff had written enough songs for another album, but we knew from experience that while they were doing what they did best, we were losing some of our identity. We were honored to be a part of the Philly family, but that wasn't enough for us. We were determined to do all of the things we had wanted to do for so many years. That's why we had to go back into our Encino studio and work together again as a family.

Going Places, our second album for Epic, was different from our first. There were more songs with messages and not as many dance songs. We knew that the message to promote peace and let music take over was a good one, but again it was more like the old O'Jays' "Love Train" and not really our style.

Still, maybe it wasn't a bad thing that there was no big pop hit on *Going Places* because it made "Different Kind of Lady" an obvious choice for club play. It was positioned in the middle of side one, so there were two Gamble and Huff songs sandwiching it, and our song stood out like a ball of fire. That was a real band cooking, with the Philly horns giving it one exclamation point after another, just as we'd hoped. That's the feel we were trying for when we were making demos with our old friend Bobby Taylor before going to Epic. Kenny and Leon put the finishing

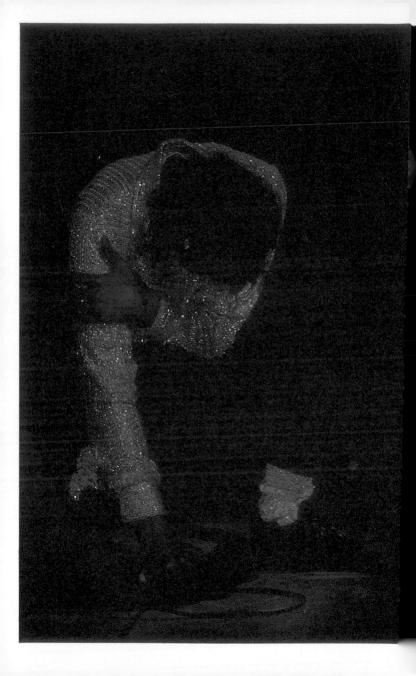

touches on it, the icing, but on this one we'd baked the cake ourselves.

After *Going Places* was in the stores, Dad asked me to accompany him to a meeting with Ron Alexenburg. Ron signed us for CBS, and he really believed in us. We wanted to convince him that we were ready now to take charge of our own music. We felt that CBS had evidence of what we could do on our own, so we stated our case, explaining that we'd originally wanted Bobby Taylor to work with us. Bobby had stuck with us through all those years, and we had thought he'd be a fine producer for us. Epic wanted Gamble and Huff because they had the track record, but maybe they were the wrong jockeys or we were the wrong horses for them, because we were letting them down in the sales department through no fault of our own. We had a strong work ethic that backed up everything we did.

Mr. Alexenburg was certainly used to dealing with performers, although I'm sure that among his business friends he could be just as cutting about musicians as we musicians could be when we were swapping our own stories among ourselves. But Dad and I were on the same wavelength when it came to the business side of music. People who make music and people who sell records are not natural enemies. I care as much about what I do as a classical musician, and I want what I do to reach the widest possible audience. The record people care about their artists, and they want to reach the widest market. As we sat in the CBS boardroom eating a nicely catered lunch, we told Mr. Alexenburg that Epic had done its best, and it wasn't good enough. We felt we could do better, that our reputation was worth putting on the line.

When we left that skyscraper known as Black Rock, Dad and I didn't say much to each other. The ride back to the hotel was a silent one, with each of us thinking our own thoughts. There wasn't much to add to what we had already said. Our whole lives had been leading to that single, important confrontation, however civilized and aboveboard it was. Maybe Ron Alexenburg has had reason to smile over the years when he remembers that day.

When that meeting took place at CBS headquarters in New York, I was only nineteen years old. I was carrying a heavy burden for nineteen. My family was relying on me more and more as far as business and creative decisions were concerned, and I was so worried about trying to do the right thing for them; but I also had an opportunity to do something I'd wanted to do all my life—act in a film. Ironically the old Motown connection was paying a late dividend.

Motown had bought the rights to film the Broadway show known as *The Wiz* even as we were leaving the company. *The Wiz* was an updated, black-oriented version of the great movie *The Wizard of Oz*, which I had always loved. I remember that when I was a kid *The Wizard of Oz* was shown on television once a year and always on a Sunday night. Kids today can't imagine what a big event that was for all of us because they've grown up with videocassettes and the expanded viewing that cable provides.

I had seen the Broadway show too, which was certainly no letdown. I swear I saw it six or seven times. I later became very friendly with the star of the show, Stephanie Mills, the Broadway Dorothy. I told her then, and I've always believed since, that it was a tragedy that her performance in the play could not have been preserved on film. I cried time after time. As much as I like the Broadway stage, I don't think I'd want to play on it myself. When you give a performance, whether on record or on film, you want to be able to judge what you've done, to measure yourself and try to improve. You can't do that in an untaped or unrecorded performance. It makes me sad to think of all the great actors who have played roles we would give anything to see, but they're lost to us because they couldn't be, or simply weren't, recorded.

If I had been tempted to go onstage, it would probably have been to work with Stephanie, although her performances were so moving that I might have cried right there in front of the audience. Motown bought *The Wiz* for one reason, and as far as I was concerned, it was the best reason possible: Diana Ross.

Diana was close to Berry Gordy and had her loyalties to him and to Motown, but she did not forget us just because our records now had a different label on them. We had been in touch throughout the changes, and she had even met up with us in Las Vegas, where she gave us tips during our run there. Diana was going to play Dorothy, and since it was the only part that was definitely cast, she encouraged me to audition. She also assured me that Motown would not keep me from getting a part just to spite me or my family. She would make sure of that if she had to, but she didn't think she'd have to.

She didn't. It was Berry Gordy who said he hoped I'd audition for *The Wiz*. I was very fortunate he felt that way, because I was bitten by the acting bug during that experience. I said to myself, *this* is what I'm interested in doing when I have a chance—this is it. When you make a film, you're capturing something elusive and you're stopping time. The people, their performances, the story become a thing that can be shared by people all over the world for generations and generations. Imagine never having seen *Captains Courageous* or *To Kill a Mockingbird*! Making movies is exciting work. It's such a team effort and it's also a lot of fun. Someday soon I plan to devote a lot of my time to making films.

I auditioned for the part of the Scarecrow because I thought his character best fit my style. I was too bouncy for the Tin Man and too light for the Lion, so I had a definite goal, and I tried to put a lot of thought into my reading and dancing for the part. When I got the call back from the director, Sidney Lumet, I felt so proud but also a little scared. The process of making a film was new to me, and I was going to have to let go of my responsibilities to my family and my music for months. I had visited New York, where we were shooting, to get the feel for Harlem that *The Wiz*'s story called for, but I had never lived there. I was surprised by how quickly I got used to the lifestyle. I enjoyed meeting a whole group of people I'd always heard about on the other coast but had never laid eyes on.

Making *The Wiz* was an education for me on so many levels. As a recording artist I already felt like an old pro, but the film world was completely new to me. I watched as closely as I could and learned a lot.

During this period in my life, I was searching, both consciously and unconsciously. I was feeling some stress and anxiety about what I wanted to do with my life now that I was an adult. I was analyzing my options and preparing to make decisions that could have a lot of repercussions. Being on the set of *The Wiz* was like being in a big school. My complexion was still a mess during the filming of the movie, so I found myself really enjoying the makeup. It was an amazing makeup job. Mine took five hours to do, six days a week; we didn't shoot on Sundays. We finally got it down to four hours flat after doing it long enough. The other people who were being made up were amazed that I didn't mind sitting there having this done for such long periods of time. They hated it, but I enjoyed having the stuff put on my face. When I was transformed into the Scarecrow, it was the most wonderful thing in the world. I got to be somebody else and escape through my character. Kids would come visit the set, and I'd have such fun playing with them and responding to them as the Scarecrow.

I'd always pictured myself doing something very elegant in the movies, but it was my experience with the makeup and costume and prop people in New York that made me realize another aspect of how wonderful filmmaking could be. I had always loved the Charlie Chaplin movies, and no one ever saw him doing anything overtly elegant in the silent movie days. I wanted something of the quality of his characters in my Scarecrow. I loved everything about the costume, from the coil legs to the tomato nose to the fright wig. I even kept the orange and white sweater that came with it and used it in a picture session years later.

The film had marvelous, very complicated dance numbers, and learning them was no problem. But that in itself became an unexpected problem with my costars.

Ever since I was a very little boy, I've been able to watch somebody do a dance step and then immediately know how to do it. Another person might have to be taken through the movement step by step and told to count and put this leg here and the hip to the right. When your hip goes to the left, put your neck over there . . . that sort of thing. But if I see it, I can do it.

When we were doing *The Wiz*, I was being instructed in the choreography along with my costars—the Tin Man, the Lion, and Diana Ross—and they were getting mad at me. I couldn't figure out what was wrong until Diana took me aside and told me that I was embarrassing her. I just stared at her. Embarrassing Diana Ross? Me? She said she knew I wasn't aware of it, but I was learning the dances much too quickly. It was embarrassing for her and the others, who just couldn't learn steps as soon as they saw the choreographer do them. She said he'd show us something and I'd just go out there and do it. When he asked the others to do it, it took them longer to learn. We laughed about it, but I tried to make the ease with which I learned my steps less obvious.

I also learned that there could be a slightly vicious side to the business of making a movie. Often when I was in front of the camera, trying to do a serious scene, one of the other characters would start making faces at me, trying to crack me up. I had always been drilled in serious professionalism and preparedness and therefore I thought it was a pretty mean thing to do. This actor would know that I had important lines to say that day, yet he would make these really crazy faces to distract me. I felt it was more than inconsiderate and unfair.

Much later Marlon Brando would tell me that people used to do that to him all the time.

The problems on the set were really few and far between and it was great working with Diana so closely. She's such a beautiful, talented woman. Doing this movie together was very special for me. I love her very much. I have always loved her very much.

The whole *Wiz* period was a time of stress and anxiety, even though I was enjoying myself. I remember July 4 of that year very well, because I was on the beach at my brother Jermaine's house, about half a block away along the waterfront. I was messing around in the surf, and all of a sudden I couldn't breathe. No air. Nothing. I asked myself what's wrong? I tried not to panic, but I ran back to the house to find Jermaine, who took me to the hospital. It was wild. A blood vessel had burst in my lung. It has never reoccurred, although I used to feel little pinches and jerks in there that were probably my imagination. I later learned that this condition was related to pleurisy. It was suggested by my doctor that I try to take things a little slower, but my schedule would not permit it. Hard work continued to be the name of the game.

As much as I liked the old *Wizard of Oz,* this new script, which differed from the Broadway production in scope rather than spirit, asked more questions than the original movie and answered them too. The atmosphere of the old movie was that of a magic kingdom sort of fairy tale. Our movie, on the other hand, had sets based on realities that kids could identify with, like schoolyards, subway stations, and the real neighborhood that our Dorothy came from. I still enjoy seeing *The Wiz* and reliving the experience. I am especially fond of the scene where Diana asks, "What am I afraid of? Don't know what I'm made of . . ." because I've felt that way many times, even during the good moments of my life. She sings about overcoming fear and walking straight and tall. She knows and the audience knows that no threat of danger can hold her back.

My character had plenty to say and to learn. I was propped up on my pole with a bunch of crows laughing at me, while I sang "You Can't Win." The song was about humiliation and helplessness—something that so many people have felt at one time or another—and the feeling that there are people out there who don't actively hold you back as much as they work quietly on your insecurities so that you hold *yourself* back. The script was clever and showed me pulling bits of information and quotations out of my straw while not really knowing how to use them. My straw contained all the answers, but I didn't know the questions.

The great difference between the two *Wizard* movies was that all the answers are given to Dorothy by the Good Witch and by her friends in Oz in the original, while in our version Dorothy comes to her own conclusions. Her loyalty to her three friends and her courage in fighting Elvina in that amazing sweatshop scene make Dorothy a memorable character. Diana's singing and dancing and acting have stayed with me ever since. She was a perfect Dorothy. After the evil witch had been defeated, the sheer joy of our dancing took over. To dance with Diana in

that movie was like an abridged version of my own story
—my knock-kneed walk and "bigfoot" spin were me in
my early days; our tabletop dance in the sweatshop scene
was where we were right then. Everything was onward
and upward. When I told my brothers and father I had
gotten this part, they thought it might be too much for
me, but the opposite was true. *The Wiz* gave me new
inspiration and strength. The question became what to do
with those things. How could I best harness them?

As I was asking myself what I wanted to do next, another
man and I were traveling parallel paths that would con-
verge on the set of *The Wiz*. We were in Brooklyn rehearsing one day, and we were reading our parts out loud to
one another. I had thought that learning lines would be
the most difficult thing I'd ever do, but I was pleasantly
surprised. Everyone had been kind, assuring me that it
was easier than I thought. And it was.

We were doing the crows' scene that day. The other
guys wouldn't even have their heads visible in this scene
because they'd be in crow costumes. They seemed to
know their parts backward and forward. I'd studied mine
too, but I hadn't said them aloud more than once or twice.

The directions called for me to pull a piece of paper
from my straw and read it. It was a quote. The author's

name, Socrates, was printed at the end. I had read Socrates, but I had never pronounced his name, so I said, "Sohcrates," because that's the way I had always assumed it was pronounced. There was a moment's silence before I heard someone whisper, "Soc-ruh-teeze." I looked over at this man I vaguely recognized. He was not one of the actors, but he seemed to belong there. I remember thinking he looked very self-confident and had a friendly face.

I smiled, a little embarrassed at having mispronounced the name, and thanked him for his help. His face was naggingly familiar, and I was suddenly sure that I had met him before. He confirmed my suspicions by extending his hand.

"Quincy Jones. I'm doing the score."

CHAPTER

FOUR

ME AND Q

I had actually first met Quincy Jones in Los Angeles when I was about twelve years old. Quincy later told me that at the time Sammy Davis, Jr., had said to him, "This kid is gonna be the next biggest thing since sliced bread." Something like that, anyway, and Quincy said, "Oh yeah?" I was little at the time, but I vaguely remember Sammy Davis introducing me to Q.

Our friendship really began to blossom on the set of *The Wiz*, and it developed into a father-and-son relationship. After *The Wiz* I called him and said, "Look, I'm going to do an album—do you think you could recommend some producers?"

I wasn't hinting. My question was a naïve but honest

one. We talked about music for a while, and, after coming up with some names and some half-hearted hemming and hawing, he said, "Why don't you let me do it?"

I really hadn't thought of it. It sounded to him as if I was hinting, but I wasn't. I just didn't think he would be that interested in my music. So I stammered something like, "Oh sure, great idea. I never thought about that."

Quincy still kids me about it.

Anyway, we immediately began to plan the album that became *Off the Wall*.

My brothers and I decided to form our own production company, and we began thinking about names to call it.

You don't find many articles about peacocks in the newspaper, but around this time I found the only one that mattered. I had always thought peacocks were beautiful and had admired one that Berry Gordy had at one of his homes. So when I read the article, which had an accompanying picture of a peacock, and revealed a great deal about the bird's characteristics, I was excited. I thought I might have found the image we were looking for. It was an in-depth piece, a little dry in places, but interesting. The writer said that the peacock's full plumage would explode only when it was in love, and then all the colors would shine—all the colors of the rainbow on one body.

I was immediately taken with that beautiful image and the meaning behind it. That bird's plumage conveyed the message I was looking for to explain the Jacksons and our intense devotion to one another, as well as our multifaceted interests. My brothers liked the idea, so we called our new company Peacock Productions, to sidestep the trap of relying too heavily on the Jackson name. Our first world tour had focused our interest in uniting people of all races through music. Some people we knew wondered what we meant when we talked about uniting all the races through music—after all, we were black musicians. Our answer was "music is color-blind." We saw that every night, especially in Europe and the other parts of the world we had visited. The people we met there loved our music. It didn't matter to them what color our skin was or which country we called home.

We wanted to form our own production company because we wanted to grow and establish ourselves as a new presence in the music world, not just as singers and dancers, but as writers, composers, arrangers, producers, and even publishers. We were interested in so many things, and we needed an umbrella company to keep track of our projects. CBS had agreed to let us produce our own album—the last two albums had sold well, but "Different Kind of Lady" showed a potential that they agreed was worth letting us develop. They did have one condition for us: they assigned an A&R man, Bobby Colomby, who used to be with Blood, Sweat, and Tears, to check in with us from time to time to see how we were doing and to see if we needed any help. We knew that the five of us needed some outside musicians to get the best possible sound, and we were weak in two areas: the keyboard and arranging sides of things. We had been faithfully adding all the new technology to our Encino studio without really having a mastery of it. Greg Phillinganes was young for a studio pro, but that was a plus as far as we were concerned because we wanted someone who would be more open to newer ways of doing things than the seasoned veterans we had encountered over the years.

He came to Encino to do preproduction work, and we all took turns surprising each other. Our mutual preconceptions just dissolved. It was a great thing to watch. As we sketched out our new songs for him, we told him that we liked the vocal tracks that Philly International always put a premium on, but when the mix came out, we always seemed to be fighting someone else's wall of sound, all those strings and cymbals. We wanted to sound cleaner and more funky, with a flintier bass and sharper horn parts. With his beautiful rhythm arrangements, Greg put into musical form what we were sketching for him and then some. We felt he was reading our minds.

A Bobby Colomby recruit who came to work with us then was Paulinho de Costa, whom we worried about because it seemed to us that Randy was being told he couldn't handle all the percussion by himself. But Paulinho brought with him the Brazilian samba tradition of adapting and improvising on primitive and often home-made instruments. When de Costa's sound joined forces with Randy's more conventional approach, we seemed to have the whole world covered.

Artistically speaking we were caught between a rock and a hard place. We had worked with the smartest, hippest pop people in the world at Motown and Philly International, and we would have been fools to discount the things we'd absorbed from them, yet we couldn't be imitators. Fortunately we got a running start with a song that Bobby Colomby brought us called "Blame It on the Boogie." It was an up-tempo, finger-poppin'-time song that was a good vehicle for the band approach we wanted to cultivate. I had fun slurring the chorus: "Blame It on the Boogie" could be sung in one breath without putting my lips together. We had a little fun with the credits on the inner sleeve of the record; "Blame It on the Boogie" was written by three guys from England, including one named Michael Jackson. It was a startling coincidence. As it turned out, writing disco songs was a natural for me because I was used to having dance breaks incorporated into all the major songs I was asked to sing.

There was a lot of uncertainty and excitement about our future. We were going through a lot of creative and personal changes—our music, the family dynamics, our desires and goals. All of this made me think more seriously about how I was spending my life, especially in relation to other people my age. I had always shouldered a lot of responsibility, but it suddenly seemed that everyone wanted a piece of me. There wasn't that much to go around, and I needed to be responsible to myself. I had to take stock of my life and figure out what people wanted from me and to whom I was going to give wholly. It was a hard thing for me to do, but I had to learn to be wary of some of the people around me. God was at the top of my list of priorities, and my mother and father and brothers and sisters followed. I was reminded of that old song by Clarence Carter called "Patches," where the oldest son is asked to take care of the farm after his father dies and his mother tells him she's depending on him. Well, we weren't sharecroppers and I wasn't the oldest, but those were slim shoulders on which to place such burdens. For some reason I always found it very difficult to say no to my family and the other people I loved. I would be asked to do something or take care of something and I would agree, even if I worried that it might be more than I could handle.

I felt under a great deal of stress and I was often emotional. Stress can be a terrible thing; you can't keep your emotions bottled up for long. There were a lot of people at this time who wondered just how committed I was to music after learning of my newfound interest in movies after being in one. It was hinted that my decision to audition had come at a bad time for the new band setup. It seemed, to outsiders, to come just as we were about to get started. But of course it worked out just fine.

"That's What You Get for Being Polite" was my way of letting on that I knew I wasn't living in an ivory tower and that I had insecurities and doubts just as all older teenagers do. I was worried that the world and all it had to offer could be passing me by even as I tried to get on top of my field.

There was a Gamble and Huff song called "Dreamer" on the first Epic album which had this theme, and as I was learning it, I felt they could have written it with me in mind. I have always been a dreamer. I set goals for myself. I look at things and try to imagine what is possible and then hope to surpass those boundaries.

In 1979 I turned twenty-one years old and began to take full control of my career. My father's personal management contract with me ran out around this time, and although it was a hard decision, the contract was not renewed.

Trying to fire your dad is not easy.

But I just didn't like the way certain things were being handled. Mixing family and business can be a delicate situation. It can be great or it can be awful; it depends on the relationships. Even at the best of times it's a hard thing to do.

Did it change the relationship between me and my father? I don't know if it did in his heart, but it certainly didn't in mine. It was a move I knew I had to make because at the time I was beginning to feel that I was working for *him* rather than that he was working for *me*. And on the creative side we are of two completely different minds. He would come up with ideas that I would totally disagree with because they weren't right for me. All I wanted was control over my own life. And I took it. I had to do it. Everyone comes to that point, sooner or later, and I had been in the business for a long time. I was pretty experienced for twenty-one—a fifteen-year veteran.

We were eager to take the *Destiny* band and concept on the road, but I got hoarse from too many shows, too much singing. When we had to cancel some performances, no one held it against me, but I felt as if I was holding my brothers back after the great job they had done while we worked together to get us all back on track. We made some makeshift adjustments in order to ease the strain on my throat. Marlon took over for me in some passages that required holding long notes. "Shake Your Body (Down to the Ground)," our set piece on the album, turned out to be a lifesaver for us onstage because we already had a good jam in the studio to build on. It was frustrating to have finally realized our dream of having our own music as the showpiece, rather than the novelty song, and not being able to give it our very best shot. It wasn't long, however, before our time would come.

In looking back, I realize I was more patient than perhaps my brothers wanted me to be. As we were remixing *Destiny*, it occurred to me that we had "left out" some things that I hadn't talked to my brothers about because I wasn't sure they'd be as interested in them as I was. Epic had arranged in the contract that they would handle any solo album I might decide to do. Perhaps they were hedging their bets; if the Jacksons couldn't make their new sound work, they could try to turn me into something they could mold for the rest of my life. That might seem like a suspicious way of thinking, but I knew from experience that money people always want to know what is going on and what can happen and how to recoup their investment. It seemed logical for them to think that way. In the light of what's happened since, I wonder about those thoughts I had, but they were real at the time.

Destiny was our biggest success as an album, and we knew we had really reached the point where people bought your record because they knew you were good and knew you'd give them your very best on every song and every album. I wanted my first solo album to be the best it could be.

I didn't want *Off the Wall* to sound like outtakes from *Destiny*. That's why I wanted to hire an outside producer who wouldn't come to this project with any preconceived notions about how it should sound. I also needed someone with a good ear to help me choose material because I didn't have enough time to write two sides of songs I'd be proud of. I knew the public expected more than two good singles on an album, especially in the discos with their extended cuts, and I wanted the fans to feel satisfied.

These are all reasons why Quincy proved to be the best producer I could have asked for. Quincy Jones's friends called him "Q" for short because of a love he has for barbecue. Later, after we'd finished *Off the Wall*, he invited me to a concert of his orchestral music at the Hollywood Bowl, but I was so shy at the time that I stood in the wings to watch the show as I had as a child. He said he expected more from me than that, and we've been trying to live up to each other's standards ever since.

That day I called to ask his advice about a producer, he started talking about people in the business—who I could work with and who I'd have trouble with. He knew track records, who was booked, who'd be too lax, who'd put the "pedal to the metal." He knew Los Angeles better than Mayor Bradley, and that's how he kept up with what was going on. As a jazz arranger, orchestrator, and film composer, someone people thought was on the outside looking in as far as pop music was concerned, he was an invaluable guide. I was so glad that my outside source was a good friend who also happened to be *the* perfect choice for a producer. He had a world of talent to choose from among his contacts, and he was a good listener, as well as a brilliant man.

The *Off the Wall* album was originally going to be called *Girlfriend*. Paul and Linda McCartney wrote a song of that title with me in mind before they ever met me.

Paul McCartney always tells people this story about me calling him and saying we should write some hit songs together.

But that's not exactly how we first met.

I saw Paul for the first time at a party on the *Queen Mary,* which is docked in Long Beach. His daughter Heather got my number from someone and gave me a call to invite me to this big party. She liked our music and we got to talking. Much later, when his Wings over America tour was completed, Paul and his family were in Los Angeles. They invited me to a party at the Harold Lloyd estate. Paul McCartney and I first met at that party. We shook hands amid a huge crowd of people, and he said, "You know, I've written a song for you." I was very surprised and thanked him. And he started singing "Girlfriend" to me at this party.

So we exchanged phone numbers and promised to get together soon, but different projects and life just got in the way for both of us and we didn't talk again for a couple of years. He ended up putting the song on his own album *London Town.*

The strangest thing happened when we were making *Off the Wall;* Quincy walked up to me one day and said, "Michael, I've got a song that's perfect for you." He played "Girlfriend" for me, not realizing, of course, that

Paul had written it for me originally. When I told him, he was astonished and pleased. We recorded it soon after and put it on the album. It was an incredible coincidence.

Quincy and I talked about *Off the Wall* and carefully planned the kind of sound we wanted. When he asked me what I most wanted to have happen in the studio, I told him, we've got to make it sound different from the Jacksons. Hard words to spit out, considering how hard we'd worked to *become* the Jacksons, but Quincy knew what I meant, and together we created an album that reflected our goal. "Rock with You," the big hit single, was the sort of thing I was aiming for. It was perfect for me to sing, and move to. Rod Temperton, whom Quincy had known because of his work with the group Heatwave on "Boogie Nights," had written the song with a more relentless, get-down arrangement in mind, but Quincy softened the attack and slipped in a synthesizer that sounded like a conch shell's insides on a beach. Q and I were both very fond of Rod's work, and we eventually asked him to work on stylizing three of his songs for me, including the title cut. Rod was a kindred spirit in many ways. Like me, he felt more at home singing and writing about the night life than actually going out and living it. It always surprises me when people assume that something an artist has created is based on a true experience or reflects his or her own lifestyle. Often nothing could be farther from the truth. I know I draw on my experiences at times, but I also hear and read things that trigger an idea for a song. An artist's imagination is his greatest tool. It can create a mood or feeling that people want to have, as well as transport you to a different place altogether.

In the studio Quincy allowed the arrangers and musicians quite a bit of freedom to express themselves, perhaps with the exception of the orchestral arrangements, which are his forte. I brought Greg Phillinganes, a member of the *Destiny* team, over to "run the floor" on numbers that he and I had worked on together in Encino, while the studio people were being lined up for the date. In addition to Greg, Paulinho da Costa was back on percussion and Randy made a cameo appearance on "Don't Stop Till You Get Enough."

Quincy is amazing and doesn't just pick yes-men to do his bidding. I have been around professionals all my life, and I can tell who is trying to keep up, who can create, and who is capable of crossing swords once in a while in a constructive way without losing sight of the shared goal. We had Louis "Thunder Thumbs" Johnson, who had worked with Quincy on the Brothers Johnson albums. We also had an all-star team of Wah Wah Watson, Marlo Henderson, David Williams, and Larry Carlton from the Crusaders playing guitar on the album. George Duke, Phil Upchurch, and Richard Heath were picked from the cream of the jazz/funk crop, and yet they never let on that maybe this music was a little different from what they were used to. Quincy and I had a good working relationship, so we shared responsibilities and consulted with one another constantly.

The Brothers Johnson notwithstanding, Quincy hadn't done much dance music before *Off the Wall*, so on "Don't Stop Till You Get Enough," "Working Day and Night," and "Get on the Floor" Greg and I worked together to build a thicker wall of sound in Quincy's studio. "Get on the Floor," though it wasn't a single, was particularly satisfying because Louis Johnson gave me a smooth-enough bottom to ride in the verses and let me come back stronger and stronger with each chorus. Bruce Swedien, Quincy's engineer, put the final touches on that mix, and I still get pleasure out of hearing it.

"Working Day and Night" was Paulinho's showcase, with my background vocals hurrying to keep up with his grab bag of toys. Greg set up a prepared electric piano with the timbre of a perfect acoustic one, to knock out any lingering echo. The lyrical theme was similar to "The Things I Do for You" from *Destiny*, but since this was a refinement of something I'd said earlier, I wanted to keep it simple and let the music put the song over the top.

"Don't Stop Till You Get Enough" had a spoken intro over bass, partly to build up tension and surprise people with the swirling strings and percussion. It was also unusual because of my vocal arrangement. On that cut I sing in overdubs as a kind of group. I wrote myself a high part, one that my solo voice couldn't carry on its own, to fit in with the music I was hearing in my head, so I let the arrangement take over from the singing. Q's fade at the end was amazing, with guitars chopping like kalimbas, the African thumb pianos. That song means a lot to me because it was the first song I wrote as a whole. "Don't Stop Till You Get Enough" was my first big chance, and it went straight to number one. It was the song that won me my first Grammy. Quincy had the confidence in me to encourage me to go into the studio by myself, which I appreciated. Then he added strings, which put icing on the cake.

The ballads were what made *Off the Wall* a Michael Jackson album. I'd done ballads with the brothers, but they had never been too enthusiastic about them and did them more as a concession to me than anything else. *Off the Wall* had, in addition to "Girlfriend," a slippery, engaging melody called "I Can't Help It" which was memorable and great fun to sing but a little quirkier than a gentle song like, say, "Rock with You."

Two of the biggest hits were "Off the Wall" and "Rock with You." You know, so much up-tempo dance music is threatening, but I liked the coaxing, the gentleness, taking a shy girl and letting her shed her fears rather than forcing them out of her. On *Off the Wall* I went back to a high-pitched voice, but "Rock with You" called for a more natural sound. I felt that if you were having a party, those two songs would get people in the door, and the harder boogie songs would send everyone home in a good mood. And then there was "She's Out of My Life." Maybe that was too personal for a party.

It was for me. Sometimes it's hard for me to look my dates in the eye even if I know them well. My dating and relationships with girls have not had the happy ending I've been looking for. Something always seems to get in the way. The things I share with millions of people aren't the sort of things you share with one. Many girls want to know what makes me tick—why I live the way I live or do the things I do—trying to get inside my head. They want to rescue me from loneliness, but they do it in such a way that they give me the impression they want to share my loneliness, which I wouldn't wish on anybody, because I believe I'm one of the loneliest people in the world.

"She's Out of My Life" is about knowing that the barriers that have separated me from others are temptingly low and seemingly easy to jump over and yet they remain standing while what I really desire disappears from my sight. Tom Bahler composed a beautiful bridge, which seemed right out of an old Broadway musical. In reality, such problems are not so easily resolved and the song presents this fact, that the problem is not overcome. We couldn't put this cut at the beginning or the end of the record, because it would have been such a downer. That's why when Stevie's song comes on afterward, so gently and tentatively, as if it was opening a door that had been bolted shut, I still go, "Whew." By the time Rod's "Burn This Disco Out" closes the record, the trance is broken.

But I got too wrapped up in "She's Out of My Life." In this case, the story's true—I cried at the end of a take, because the words suddenly had such a strong effect on me. I had been letting so much build up inside me. I was twenty-one years old, and I was so rich in some experiences while being poor in moments of true joy. Sometimes I imagine that my life experience is like an image in one of those trick mirrors in the circus, fat in one part and thin to the point of disappearing in another. I was worried that would show up on "She's Out of My Life," but if it touched people's heartstrings, knowing that would make me feel less lonely.

When I got emotional after that take, the only people with me were Q and Bruce Swedien. I remember burying my face in my hands and hearing only the hum of the machinery as my sobs echoed in the room. Later I apologized, but they said there was no need.

Making *Off the Wall* was one of the most difficult periods of my life, despite the eventual success it enjoyed. I had very few close friends at the time and felt very isolated. I was so lonely that I used to walk through my neighborhood hoping I'd run into somebody I could talk to and perhaps become friends with. I wanted to meet people who didn't know who I was. I wanted to run into somebody who would be my friend because they liked me and needed a friend too, not because I was who I am. I wanted to meet *anybody* in the neighborhood—the neighborhood kids, anybody.

Success definitely brings on loneliness. It's true. People think you're lucky, that you have everything. They think you can go anywhere and do anything, but that's not the point. One hungers for the basic stuff.

I've learned to cope better with these things now and I don't get nearly as depressed as I used to.

I didn't really have any girlfriends when I was in school. There were girls I thought were cute, but I found it so difficult to approach them. I was too embarrassed—I don't know why—it was just crazy. There was one girl who was a good friend to me. I liked her, but I was too embarrassed to tell her.

My first real date was with Tatum O'Neal. We met at a club on Sunset Strip called On the Rox. We exchanged phone numbers and called each other often. I talked to her for hours: from the road, from the studio, from home. On our first date we went to a party at Hugh Hefner's Playboy Mansion and had a great time. She had held my hand for the first time that night at On the Rox. When we met, I was sitting at this table and all of a sudden I felt this soft hand reach over and grab mine. It was Tatum. This probably wouldn't mean a lot to other people, but it was serious stuff to me. *She touched me.* That's how I felt about it. In the past, girls had always touched me on tour; grabbing at me and screaming, behind a wall of security guards. But this was different, this was one-on-one, and that's always the best.

Ours developed into a real close relationship. I fell in love with her (and she with me) and we were very close for a long time. Eventually the relationship transcended into a good friendship. We still talk now and then, and I guess you'd have to say she was my first love—after Diana.

When I heard Diana Ross was getting married, I was happy for her because I knew it would make her very joyous. Still, it was hard for me, because I had to walk around pretending to be overwhelmed that Diana was getting married to this man I'd never met. I wanted her to be happy, but I have to admit that I was a bit hurt and a little jealous because I've always loved Diana and always will.

Another love was Brooke Shields. We were romantically serious for a while. There have been a lot of wonderful women in my life, women whose names wouldn't mean anything to the readers of this book, and it would be unfair to discuss them because they are not celebrities and are unaccustomed to having their names in print. I value my privacy and therefore I respect theirs as well.

Liza Minelli is a person whose friendship I'll always cherish. She's like my show business sister. We get together and talk about the business; it comes out of our pores. We both eat, sleep, and drink various moves and songs and dance. We have the best time together. I love her.

Right after we finished *Off the Wall*, I plunged into making the *Triumph* album with my brothers. We wanted to combine the best of both albums for our tour. "Can You Feel It?" was the first cut on the album, and it had the closest thing to a rock feel that the Jacksons had ever done. It wasn't really dance music either. We had it in mind for the video that opened our tour, kind of like our own *Also Sprach Zarathustra,* the *2001* theme. Jackie and I had thought of combining the band sound with a gospel/children's choir feel. That was a nod to Gamble and Huff, in a way, because the song was a celebration of love taking over, cleansing the sins of the world. Randy's singing is so good, even if his range is not all he'd like it to be. His breathing and phrasing kept me pumped up on my toes when we sang it. There was a bright foghorn-type keyboard that I worked on for hours, going over it and over it again, until I got it the way I wanted it. We had six minutes, and I don't think it was one second too long.

"Lovely One" was an extension of "Shake Your Body Down to the Ground," with that lighter *Off the Wall* sound injected. I tried out a newer, more ethereal voice on Jackie's "Your Ways," with the keyboards adding a faraway quality. Paulinho brought out all the artillery: triangles, skulls, gongs. This song's about a strange girl who is the way she is and there's nothing I can do about it, other than enjoy it when I can.

"Everybody" is more playful than the *Off the Wall*

dance tunes, with Mike McKinney propelling it like a plane turning and bearing down. The background vocals suggest "Get on the Floor's" influence, but Quincy's sound is deeper, like you're in the eye of the storm—our sound was more like going up the glass elevator to the top floor while looking down, rising effortlessly.

"Time Waits for No One" was written by Jackie and Randy with my voice and style in mind. They knew they were trying to keep up with the *Off the Wall* songwriters and they did a very good job. "Give It Up" gave everyone a chance to sing, Marlon in particular. We strayed from the band sound on those tracks, perhaps sinking back into that Philly trap of letting the arrangement overwhelm us. "Walk Right Now" and "Wondering Who" were closer to the *Destiny* sound, but for the most part they were suffering from too many cooks and not enough broth.

There was one exception: "Heartbreak Hotel." I swear that was a phrase that came out of my head and I wasn't thinking of any other song when I wrote it. The record company printed it on the cover as "This Place Hotel," because of the Elvis Presley connection. As important as he was to music, black as well as white, he just wasn't an influence on me. I guess he was too early for me. Maybe it was timing more than anything else. By the time our song had come out, people thought that if I kept living in seclusion the way I was, I might die the way he did. The parallels aren't there as far as I'm concerned and I was never much for scare tactics. Still, the way Elvis destroyed himself interests me, because I don't ever want to walk those grounds myself.

LaToya was asked to contribute the scream that opens the song—not the most auspicious start to a recording career, I'll admit, but she was just getting her feet wet in the studio. She has made some good records since and is quite accomplished. The scream was the kind that normally shatters a bad dream, but our intention was to have the dream only begin, to make the listener wonder whether it was a dream or reality. That was the effect I think we got. The three female backup singers were amused when they were doing the scary backup effects that I wanted, until they actually heard them in the mix.

"Heartbreak Hotel" was the most ambitious song I had composed. I think I worked on a number of levels: You could dance to it, sing along with it, get scared by it, and just listen. I had to tack on a slow piano and cello coda that ended on a positive note to reassure the listener; there's no point in trying to scare someone if there isn't something to bring the person back safe and sound from where you've taken them. "Heartbreak Hotel" had revenge in it and I am fascinated by the concept of revenge.

It's something I can't understand. The idea of making someone "pay" for something they've done to you or that you imagine they've done to you is totally alien to me. The setup showed my own fears and for the time being helped quell them. There were so many sharks in this business looking for blood in the water.

If this song, and later "Billie Jean," seemed to cast women in an unfavorable light, it was not meant to be taken as a personal statement. Needless to say, I love the interaction between the sexes; it is a natural part of life and I love women. I just think that when sex is used as a form of blackmail or power, it's a repugnant use of one of God's gifts

Triumph gave us that final burst of energy we needed to put together a perfect show, with no marginal material. We began rehearsing with our touring band, which included bass player Mike McKinney. David Williams would travel with us too, but he was now a permanent member of the band.

The upcoming tour was going to be a big undertaking. We had special effects arranged for us by the great magician Doug Henning. I wanted to disappear completely in a puff of smoke right after "Don't Stop." He had to coordinate the special effects with the Showco people who controlled the whole setup. I was happy to talk with him while we walked through the routine. It seemed almost unfair for him to give me his secrets, and apart from the money I wasn't offering him anything he could make use of in return. I felt a little embarrassed about that, yet I really wanted our show to be great and I knew Henning's contribution would be spectacular. We were competing with bands like Earth, Wind, and Fire and the Commodores for the position of top band in the country, and we knew there were people who felt that the Jackson brothers had been around for ten years and were finished.

I had worked hard on the concept for the set for the upcoming tour. It had the feel of *Close Encounters* behind it. I was trying to make the statement that there was life and meaning beyond space and time and the peacock had burst forth ever brighter and ever prouder. I wanted our film to reflect this idea, too.

My pride in the rhythms, the technical advances, and the success of *Off the Wall* was offset by the jolt I got when the Grammy nominations were announced for 1979. Although *Off the Wall* had been one of the most popular records of the year, it received only one nomination: Best R&B Vocal Performance. I remember where I was when I got the news. I felt ignored by my peers and it hurt. People told me later that it surprised the industry too.

I was disappointed and then I got excited thinking about the album to come. I said to myself, "Wait until next time"—they won't be able to ignore the next album. I watched the ceremony on television and it was nice to win in my category, but I was still upset by what I perceived as the rejection of my peers. I just kept thinking, "Next time, next time." In many ways an artist is his work. It's difficult to separate the two. I think I can be brutally objective about my work as I create it, and if something doesn't work, I can feel it, but when I turn in a finished album— or song—you can be sure that I've given it every ounce of energy and God-given talent that I have. *Off the Wall* was well received by my fans and I think that's why the Grammy nominations hurt. That experience lit a fire in my soul. All I could think of was the next album and what I would do with it. I wanted it to be truly great.

151

CHAPTER
FIVE

THE MOONWALK

Off the Wall was released in August 1979, the same month I turned twenty-one and took control of my own affairs, and it was definitely one of the major landmarks of my life. It meant a great deal to me, because its eventual success proved beyond a shadow of a doubt that a former "child star" could mature into a recording artist with contemporary appeal. Off the Wall also went a step beyond the dance grooves we had cooked up. When we started the project, Quincy and I talked about how important it was to capture passion and strong feelings in a recorded performance. I still think that's what we achieved on the ballad "She's Out of My Life," and to a lesser extent on "Rock with You."

Looking back, I can view the whole tapestry and see how *Off the Wall* prepared me for the work we would do on the album that became *Thriller*. Quincy, Rod Temperton, and many of the musicians who played on *Off the Wall* would help me realize a dream that I had had for a long time. *Off the Wall* had sold almost six million copies in this country, but I wanted to make an album that would be even bigger. Ever since I was a little boy, I had dreamed of creating the biggest-selling record of all time. I remember going swimming as a child and making a wish before I jumped into the pool. Remember, I grew up knowing the industry, understanding goals, and being told what was and was not possible. I wanted to do something special. I'd stretch my arms out, as if I were sending my thoughts right up into space. I'd make my wish, then I'd dive into the water. I'd say to myself, "This is my dream. This is my wish," every time before I'd dive into the water.

I believe in wishes and in a person's ability to make a wish come true. I really do. Whenever I saw a sunset, I would quietly make my secret wish right before the sun tucked under the western horizon and disappeared. It would seem as if the sun had taken my wish with it. I'd make it right before that last speck of light vanished. And a wish is more than a wish, it's a goal. It's something your conscious and subconscious can help make reality.

I remember being in the studio once with Quincy and Rod Temperton while we were working on *Thriller*. I was playing a pinball machine and one of them asked me, "If this album doesn't do as well as *Off the Wall*, will you be disappointed?"

I remember feeling upset—hurt that the question was even raised. I told them *Thriller* had to do better than *Off the Wall*. I admitted that I wanted this album to be the biggest-selling album of all time.

They started laughing. It was a seemingly unrealistic thing to want.

There were times during the *Thriller* project when I would get emotional or upset because I couldn't get the people working with me to see what I saw. That still happens to me sometimes. Often people just don't see what I see. They have too much doubt. You can't do your best when you're doubting yourself. If you don't believe in yourself, who will? Just doing as well as you did last time is not good enough. I think of it as the "Try to get what you can" mentality. It doesn't require you to stretch, to grow. I don't believe in that.

I believe we are powerful, but we don't use our minds to full capacity. Your mind is powerful enough to help you attain whatever you want. I *knew* what we could do with that record. We had a great team there, a lot of talent and good ideas, and I knew we could do anything. The success of *Thriller* transformed many of my dreams into reality. It did become the biggest-selling album of all time, and that fact appeared on the cover of *The Guinness Book of World Records.*

Making the *Thriller* album was very hard work, but it's true that you only get out of something what you put into it. I'm a perfectionist; I'll work until I drop. And I worked so hard on that album. It helped that Quincy showed great confidence in what we were doing during those sessions. I guess I had proved myself to him during our work on *Off the Wall.* He listened to what I had to say and helped me accomplish what I had hoped to on that album, but he showed even more faith in me during the making of *Thriller.* He realized I had the confidence and experience I needed to make that record and at times he wasn't in the studio with us for that reason. I'm really very self-confident when it comes to my work. When I take on a project, I believe in it 100 percent. I really put my soul into it. I'd die for it. That's how I am.

Quincy is brilliant at balancing out an album, creating the right mix of up-tempo numbers and slow ones. We started out working with Rod Temperton on songs for the

Thriller album, which was originally called *Starlight*. I was writing songs myself while Quincy was listening to other people's songs, hoping to find just the right ones for the album. He's good at knowing what I'll like and what will work for me. We both share the same philosophy about making albums; we don't believe in B-sides or album songs. Every song should be able to stand on its own as a single, and we always push for this.

I had finished some songs of my own, but I didn't give them to Quincy until I saw what had come in from other writers. The first song I had was "Startin' Something," which I had written when we were doing *Off the Wall* but had never given to Quincy for that album. Sometimes I have a song I've written that I really like and I just can't bring myself to present it. While we were making *Thriller,* I even held on to "Beat It" for a long time before I played it for Quincy. He kept telling me that we needed a great rock song for the album. He'd say, "Come on, where is it? I *know* you got it." I like my songs but initially I'm shy about playing them for people, because I'm afraid they *won't* like them and that's a painful experience.

He finally convinced me to let him hear what I had. I brought out "Beat It" and played it for him and he went crazy. I felt on top of the world.

When we were about to start work on *Thriller,* I

called Paul McCartney in London and this time I did say, "Let's get together and write some hits." Our collaboration produced "Say Say Say" and "The Girl Is Mine."

Quincy and I eventually chose "The Girl Is Mine" as the obvious first single from *Thriller.* We really didn't have much choice. When you have two strong names like that together on a song, it has to come out first or it gets played to death and overexposed. We had to get it out of the way.

When I approached Paul, I wanted to repay the favor he had done me in contributing "Girlfriend" to *Off the Wall.* I wrote "The Girl Is Mine," which I knew would be right for his voice and mine working together, and we also did work on "Say Say Say," which we would finish up later with George Martin, the great Beatles producer.

"Say Say Say" was coauthored by Paul, a man who could play all the instruments in the studio and score every part, and a kid, me, who couldn't. Yet we worked together as equals and enjoyed ourselves. Paul never had to carry me in that studio. The collaboration was also a real step forward for me in terms of confidence, because there was no Quincy Jones watching over me to correct my mistakes. Paul and I shared the same idea of how a pop song should work and it was a real treat to work with him. I feel that ever since John Lennon's death he has had to live up to expectations people had no right to hang on him; Paul McCartney has given so much to this industry and to his fans.

Eventually, I would buy the ATV music publishing catalogue, which included many of the great Lennon-McCartney songs. But most people don't know that it was Paul who introduced me to the idea of getting involved in music publishing. I was staying with Paul and Linda at their house in the country when Paul told me about his own involvement in music publishing. He handed me a little book with *MPL* printed on the cover. He smiled as I opened it, because he knew I was going to find the contents exciting. It contained a list of all the songs Paul owns and he'd been buying the rights to songs for a long time. I had never given the idea of buying songs any thought before. When the ATV music publishing catalogue, which contains many Lennon-McCartney songs, went on sale, I decided to put in a bid.

I consider myself a musician who is incidentally a businessman, and Paul and I had both learned the hard way about business and the importance of publishing and royalties and the dignity of songwriting. Songwriting should be treated as the lifeblood of popular music. The creative process doesn't involve time clocks or quota systems, it involves inspiration and the willingness to follow through. When I was sued by someone I had never heard of for "The Girl Is Mine," I was quite willing to stand on my reputation. I stated that many of my ideas come in dreams, which some people thought was a convenient cop-out, but it's true. Our industry is so lawyer-heavy that getting sued for something you didn't do seems to be as much a part of the initiation process as winning amateur night used to be.

"Not My Lover" was a title we almost used for "Billie Jean" because Q had some objections to calling the song "Billie Jean," my original title. He felt people might immediately think of Billie Jean King, the tennis player.

A lot of people have asked me about that song, and the answer is very simple. It's just a case of a girl who says that I'm the father of her child and I'm pleading my innocence because "the kid is not my son."

There was never a real "Billie Jean." (Except for the ones who came after the song.) The girl in the song is a composite of people we've been plagued by over the years. This kind of thing has happened to some of my brothers and I used to be really amazed by it. I couldn't understand how these girls could say they were carrying someone's child when it wasn't true. I can't imagine lying about something like that. Even today there are girls who come to the gate at our house and say the strangest things, like, "Oh, I'm Michael's wife," or "I'm just dropping off the keys to our apartment." I remember one girl who used to drive us completely crazy. I really think that she believed in her mind that she belonged with me. There was another girl who claimed I had gone to bed with her, and she made threats. There've been a couple of serious scuffles at the gate on Hayvenhurst, and they can get dangerous. People yell into the intercom that Jesus sent them to speak with me and God told them to come— unusual and unsettling things.

A musician knows hit material. It has to feel right. Everything has to feel in place. It fulfills you and it makes you feel good. You know it when you hear it. That's how I felt about "Billie Jean." I knew it was going to be big while I was writing it. I was really absorbed in that song. One day during a break in a recording session I was riding down the Ventura Freeway with Nelson Hayes, who was working with me at the time. "Billie Jean" was going around in my head and that's all I was thinking about. We were getting off the freeway when a kid on a motorcycle pulls up to us and says, "Your car's on fire." Suddenly we noticed the smoke and pulled over and the whole bottom of the Rolls-Royce was on fire. That kid probably saved our lives. If the car had exploded, we could have been killed.

But I was so absorbed by this tune floating in my head that I didn't even focus on the awful possibilities until later. Even while we were getting help and finding an alternate way to get where we were going, I was silently composing additional material, that's how involved I was with "Billie Jean."

Before I wrote "Beat It," I had been thinking I wanted to write the type of rock song that I would go out and buy, but also something totally different from the rock music I was hearing on Top 40 radio at the time.

"Beat It" was written with school kids in mind. I've always loved creating pieces that will appeal to kids. It's fun to write for them and know what they like because they're a very demanding audience. You can't fool them. They are still the audience that's most important to me, because I really care about them. If they like it, it's a hit, no matter what the charts say.

The lyrics of "Beat It" express something I would do if I were in trouble. Its message—that we should abhor violence—is something I believe deeply. It tells kids to be smart and avoid trouble. I don't mean to say you should turn the other cheek while someone kicks in your teeth, but, unless your back is against the wall and you have absolutely no choice, just get away before violence breaks out. If you fight and get killed, you've gained nothing and lost everything. You're the loser, and so are the people who love you. That's what "Beat It" is supposed to get across. To me true bravery is settling differences without a fight and having the wisdom to make that solution possible.

When Q called Eddie Van Halen, he thought it was a crank call. Because of the bad connection, Eddie was convinced that the voice on the other end was a fake. After being told to get lost, Q simply dialed the number again. Eddie agreed to play the session for us and gave us an incredible guitar solo on "Beat It."

The newest members of our team were the band Toto, who had the hit records "Rosanna" and "Africa." They had been well known as individual session musicians before they came together as a group. Because of their experience, they knew both sides of studio work, when to be independent, and when to be cooperative and follow the producer's lead. Steve Porcaro had worked on *Off the Wall* during a break as keyboardist for Toto. This time he brought his band mates with him. Musicologists know that the band's leader David Paich is the son of Marty Paich, who worked on Ray Charles' great records like "I Can't Stop Loving You."

I love "Pretty Young Thing," which was written by Quincy and James Ingram. "Don't Stop Till You Get Enough" had whetted my appetite for the spoken intro, partly because I didn't think my speaking voice was something my singing needed to hide. I have always had a soft speaking voice. I haven't cultivated it or chemically altered it: that's me—take it or leave it. Imagine what it must be like to be criticized for something about yourself that is natural and God given. Imagine the hurt of having untruths spread by the press, of having people wonder if you're telling the truth—defending yourself because someone decided it would make good copy and would force you to deny what they said, thus creating another story. I've tried not to answer such ridiculous charges in the past because that dignifies them and the people who make them. Remember, the press is a business: Newspapers and magazines are in business to make money— sometimes at the expense of accuracy, fairness, and even the truth.

Anyway, in the intro to "Pretty Young Thing," I sounded a bit more confident than I had on the last album. I liked the "code" in the lyrics, and "tenderoni" and "sugar fly" were fun rock 'n' roll-type words that you couldn't find in the dictionary. I got Janet and LaToya into the studio for this one, and they produced the "real"

backup vocals. James Ingram and I programmed an electronic device called a Vocoder, which gave out that E.T. voice.

"Human Nature" was the song the Toto guys brought to Q, and he and I both agreed that the song had the prettiest melody we'd heard in a long time, even more than "Africa." It's music with wings. People asked me about the lyrics: "Why does he do me that way . . . I like loving this way . . ." People often think the lyrics you're singing have some special personal significance for you, which often isn't true. It is important to reach people, to move them. Sometimes one can do this with the mosaic of the music melody arrangement and lyrics, sometimes it is the intellectual content of the lyrics. I was asked a lot of questions about "Muscles," the song I wrote and produced for Diana Ross. That song fulfilled a lifelong dream of returning some of the many favors she's done for me. I have always loved Diana and looked up to her. Muscles, by the way, is the name of my snake.

"The Lady in My Life" was one of the most difficult tracks to cut. We were used to doing a lot of takes in order to get a vocal as nearly perfect as possible, but Quincy wasn't satisfied with my work on that song, even after literally dozens of takes. Finally he took me aside late one session and told me he wanted me to beg. That's what he said. He wanted me to go back to the studio and literally *beg* for it. So I went back in and had them turn off the studio lights and close the curtain between the studio and the control room so I wouldn't feel self-conscious. Q started the tape and I begged. The result is what you hear in the grooves.

Eventually we came under tremendous pressure from our record company to finish *Thriller*. When a record company rushes you, they really rush you, and they were rushing us hard on *Thriller*. They said it had to be ready on a certain date, do or die.

So we went through a period where we were breaking our backs to get the album done by their deadline. There were a lot of compromises made on the mixes of various tracks, and on whether certain tracks were even going to be on the record. We cut so many corners that we almost lost the whole album.

When we finally listened to the tracks we were going to hand in, *Thriller* sounded so crappy to me that tears came to my eyes. We had been under enormous pressure because while we were trying to finish *Thriller* we also had been working on *The E.T. Storybook,* and there had been deadline pressure on that as well. All these people were fighting back and forth with each other, and we

came to realize that the sad truth was that the mixes of
Thriller didn't work.

We sat there in the studio, Westlake Studio in Holly-
wood, and listened to the whole album. I felt devastated.
All this pent-up emotion came out. I got angry and left the
room. I told my people, "That's it, we're not releasing it.
Call CBS and tell them they are not getting this album.
We are *not* releasing it."

Because I knew it was wrong. If we hadn't stopped
the process and examined what we were doing, the record would have been terrible. It never would have been
reviewed the way it was because, as we learned, you can
ruin a great album in the mix. It's like taking a great
movie and ruining it in the editing. You simply have to
take your time.

Some things can't be rushed.

There was a bit of yelling and screaming from the
record people, but in the end they were smart and under
stood. They knew too; it was just that I was the first to say
it. Finally I realized I had to do the whole thing—mix the
entire album—all over again.

We took a couple of days off, drew a deep breath, and
stepped back. Then we came to it fresh, cleaned our ears
out, and began to mix two songs a week. When it was done

—boom—it hit us hard. CBS could hear the difference too. *Thriller* was a tough project.

It felt so good when we finished. I was so excited I couldn't wait for it to come out. When we finished, there wasn't any kind of celebration that I can recall. We didn't go out to a disco or anything. We just rested. I prefer just being with people I really like anyway. That's my way of celebrating.

The three videos that came out of *Thriller*—"Billie Jean," "Beat It," and "Thriller"—were all part of my original concept for the album. I was determined to present this music as visually as possible. At the time I would look at what people were doing with video, and I couldn't understand why so much of it seemed so primitive and weak. I saw kids watching and accepting boring videos because they had no alternatives. My goal is to do the best I can in every area, so why work hard on an album and then produce a terrible video? I wanted something that would *glue* you to the set, something you'd want to watch over and over. The idea from the beginning was to give people quality. So I wanted to be a pioneer in this relatively new medium and make the best short music movies we could make. I don't even like to call them videos. On the set I explained that we were doing a *film,* and that was how I approached it. I wanted the most talented people in the business—the best cinematographer, the best director, the best lighting people we could get. We weren't shooting on videotape; it was 35-mm film. We were serious.

For the first video, "Billie Jean," I interviewed several directors, looking for someone who seemed really unique. Most of them didn't present me with anything that was truly innovative. At the same time I was trying to think bigger, the record company was giving me a problem on the budget. So I ended up paying for "Beat It" and "Thriller" because I didn't want to argue with anybody about money. I own both of those films myself as a result.

"Billie Jean" was done with CBS's money—about $250,000. At the time that was a lot of money for a video, but it really pleased me that they believed in me that much. Steve Baron, who directed "Billie Jean," had very imaginative ideas, although he didn't agree at first that there should be dancing in it. I felt that people wanted to see dancing. It was great to dance for the video. That freeze-frame where I go on my toes was spontaneous; so were many of the other moves.

"Billie Jean's" video made a big impression on the MTV audience and was a huge hit.

"Beat It" was directed by Bob Giraldi, who had done a lot of commercials. I remember being in England when it was decided that "Beat It" would be the next single released from *Thriller,* and we had to choose a director for the video.

I felt "Beat It" should be interpreted literally, the way it was written, one gang against another on tough urban streets. It had to be *rough.* That's what "Beat It" was about.

When I got back to L.A., I saw Bob Giraldi's demo reel and knew that he was the director I wanted for "Beat It." I loved the way he told a story in his work, so I talked with him about "Beat It." We went over things, my ideas and his ideas, and that's how it was created. We played with the storyboard and molded it and sculpted it.

I had street gangs on my mind when I wrote "Beat It," so we rounded up some of the toughest gangs in Los Angeles and put them to work on the video. It turned out to be a good idea, and a great experience for me. We had some rough kids on that set, tough kids, and they hadn't been to wardrobe. Those guys in the pool room in the first scene were serious; they were not actors. That stuff was real.

Now I hadn't been around really tough people all that much, and these guys were more than a little intimidating at first. But we had security around and were ready for anything that might happen. Of course we soon realized we didn't need any of this, that the gang members were mostly humble, sweet, and kind in their dealings with us. We fed them during breaks, and they all cleaned up and put their trays away. I came to realize that the whole thing about being bad and tough is that it's done for recognition. All along these guys had wanted to be seen and respected, and now we were going to put them on TV. They *loved* it. "Hey, look at me, I'm somebody!" And I think that's really why many of the gangs act the way they do. They're rebels, but rebels who want attention and respect. Like all of us, they just want to be seen. And I gave them that chance. For a few days at least they were stars.

They were so wonderful to me—polite, quiet, supportive. After the dance numbers they'd compliment my work, and I could tell they really meant it. They wanted a lot of autographs and frequently stood around my trailer. Whatever they wanted, I gave them: photographs, autographs, tickets for the Victory tour, anything. They were a nice bunch of guys.

The truth of that experience came out on the screen. The "Beat It" video was menacing, and you could *feel* those people's emotions. You felt the experience of the streets and the reality of their lives. You look at "Beat It" and know those kids are tough. They were being themselves, and it came across. It was nothing like actors acting; it was as far from that as possible. They were being themselves; that feeling you got was *their* spirit.

I've always wondered if they got the same message from the song that I did.

When *Thriller* first came out, the record company assumed it would sell a couple of million copies. In general record companies never believe a new album will do considerably better than the last one you did. They figure you either got lucky last time or the number you last sold is the size of your audience. They usually just ship a couple of million out to the stores to cover the sales in case you get lucky again.

That's how it usually works, but I wanted to alter their attitude with *Thriller*.

One of the people who helped me with *Thriller* was Frank Dileo. Frank was vice president for promotion at Epic when I met him. Along with Ron Weisner and Fred DeMann, Frank was responsible for turning my dream for *Thriller* into a reality. Frank heard parts of *Thriller* for the first time at Westlake Studio in Hollywood, where much of the album was recorded. He was there with Freddie DeMann, one of my managers, and Quincy and I played them "Beat It" and a little bit of "Thriller," which we

Beginning of the
world tour, 1987.

With my sister
LaToya in the
"Say Say Say" video.

left, top In Florida at
Barry Gibb's House.

middle Some of the many
awards I've been honored
to receive.

lower Having fun with
Bill Bray.

above I can't resist babies.
In China, 1987.
above right My nephew Taj
and I have some real fun.
right Arriving in Sydney,
Australia, holding a gift
from a young fan.

below In the subway, New
York City, 1987,
filming "Bad".
below right Between breaks
in filming *Smooth Criminal*
with Sean Lennon, Brandon
Adams, and Kelly Parker.

were still working on. They were very impressed, and we started to talk seriously about how to "break" this album wide open.

Frank really worked hard and proved to be my right hand during the years ahead. His brilliant understanding of the recording industry proved invaluable. For instance, we released "Beat It" as a single while "Billie Jean" was still at number one. CBS screamed, "You're crazy. This will kill 'Billie Jean.' " But Frank told them not to worry, that both songs would be number one and both would be in the Top 10 at the same time. They were.

By the spring of 1983 it was clear that the album was going to go crazy. Over the top. Every time they released another single, sales of the album would go even higher.

Then the "Beat It" video took off.

On May 16, 1983, I performed "Billie Jean" on a network telecast in honor of Motown's twenty-fifth anniversary. Almost fifty million people saw that show. After that, many things changed.

The *Motown 25* show had actually been taped a month earlier, in April. The whole title was *Motown 25: Yesterday, Today, and Forever,* and I'm forced to admit I had to be talked into doing it. I'm glad I did because the show eventually produced some of the happiest and proudest moments of my life.

As I mentioned earlier, I said no to the idea at first. I had been asked to appear as a member of the Jacksons and then to do a dance number on my own. But none of us were Motown artists any longer. There were lengthy debates between me and my managers, Weisner and DeMann. I thought about how much Berry Gordy had done for me and the group, but I told my managers and Motown that I didn't want to go on TV. My whole attitude toward TV is fairly negative. Eventually Berry came to see me to discuss it. I was editing "Beat It" at the Motown studio, and someone must have told him I was in the building. He came down to the studio and talked to me about it at length. I said, "Okay, but if I do it, I want to do 'Billie Jean.'" It would have been the only non-Motown song in the whole show. He told me that's what he wanted me to do anyway. So we agreed to do a Jacksons' medley, which would include Jermaine. We were all thrilled.

So I gathered my brothers and rehearsed them for this show. I really worked them, and it felt nice, a bit like the old days of the Jackson 5. I choreographed them and rehearsed them for *days* at our house in Encino, videotaping every rehearsal so we could watch it later. Jermaine and Marlon also made their contributions. Next we went to Motown in Pasadena for rehearsals. We did our act and, even though we reserved our energy and never went all out at rehearsal, all the people there were clapping and coming around and watching us. Then I did my "Billie Jean" rehearsal. I just walked through it because as yet I had nothing planned. I hadn't had time because I was so busy rehearsing the group.

The next day I called my management office and said, "Please order me a spy's hat, like a cool fedora—something that a secret agent would wear." I wanted something sinister and special, a real slouchy kind of hat. I still didn't have a very good idea of what I was going to do with "Billie Jean."

During the *Thriller* sessions, I had found a black jacket, and I said, "You know, someday I'm going to wear this to perform. It was so perfect and so show business that I wore it on *Motown 25.*

But the night before the taping, I still had no idea what I was going to do with my solo number. So I went down to the kitchen of our house and played "Billie Jean." Loud. I was in there by myself, the night before the show, and I pretty much stood there and let the song tell me what to do. I kind of let the dance create itself. I really let it *talk* to me; I heard the beat come in, and I took this spy's hat and started to pose and step, letting the "Billie Jean"

rhythm create the movements. I felt almost compelled to let it create itself. I couldn't help it. And that—being able to "step back" and let the dance come through—was a lot of fun.

I had also been practicing certain steps and movements, although most of the performance was actually spontaneous. I had been practicing the Moonwalk for some time, and it dawned on me in our kitchen that I would finally do the Moonwalk in public on *Motown 25*.

Now the Moonwalk was already out on the street by this time, but I enhanced it a little when I did it. It was born as a break-dance step, a "popping" type of thing that black kids had created dancing on street corners in the ghetto. Black people are truly innovative dancers; they create many of the new dances, pure and simple. So I said, "This is my chance to do it," and I did it. These three kids taught it to me. They gave me the basics—and I had been doing it a lot in private. I had practiced it together with certain other steps. All I was really sure of was that on the bridge to "Billie Jean" I was going to walk backward and forward at the same time, like walking on the moon.

On the day of the taping, Motown was running behind schedule. Late. So I went off and rehearsed by myself. By then I had my spy hat. My brothers wanted to know what the hat was for, but I told them they'd have to wait and see. But I did ask Nelson Hayes for a favor. "Nelson—after I do the set with my brothers and the lights go down, sneak the hat out to me in the dark. I'll be in the corner, next to the wings, talking to the audience, but you sneak that hat back there and put it in my hand in the dark."

So after my brothers and I finished performing, I walked over to the side of the stage and said, "You're beautiful! I'd like to say those were the good old days; those were magic moments with all my brothers, including Jermaine. But what I really like"—and Nelson is sneaking the hat into my hand—"are the newer songs." I turned around and grabbed the hat and went into "Billie Jean," into that heavy rhythm; I could tell that people in the audience were really enjoying my performance. My brothers told me they were crowding the wings watching me with their mouths open, and my parents and sisters were out there in the audience. But I just remember opening my eyes at the end of the thing and seeing this sea of people standing up, applauding. And I felt so many conflicting emotions. I knew I had done my best and felt good, so good. But at the same time I felt disappointed in myself. I had planned to do one really long spin and to stop on my toes, suspended for a moment, but I didn't stay on my toes as long as I wanted. I did the spin and I landed on one toe. I wanted to just stay there, just *freeze* there, but it didn't work quite as I'd planned.

When I got backstage, the people back there were congratulating me. I was still disappointed about the spin. I had been concentrating so hard and I'm such a perfectionist. At the same time I knew this was one of the happiest moments of my life. I knew that for the first time my brothers had really gotten a chance to watch me and see what I was doing, how I was evolving. After the performance, each of them hugged and kissed me backstage. They had never done that before, and I felt happy for all of us. It was so wonderful when they kissed me like that. I loved it! I mean, we hug all the time. My whole family embraces a lot, except for my father. He's the only one who doesn't. Whenever the rest of us see each other, we embrace, but when they all kissed me that night, I felt as if I had been blessed by them.

The performance was still gnawing at me, and I wasn't satisfied until a little boy came up to me backstage. He was about ten years old and was wearing a tuxedo. He looked up at me with stars in his eyes, frozen where he stood, and said, "Man, who ever taught you to dance like that?"

I kind of laughed and said, "Practice, I guess." And this boy was looking at me, awestruck. I walked away, and for the first time that evening I felt really good about what I had accomplished that night. I said to myself, I must have done really well because children are honest. When that kid said what he did, I really felt that I *had* done a good job, I was so moved by the whole experience that I went right home and wrote down everything which had happened that night. My entry ended with my encounter with the child.

The day after the *Motown 25* show, Fred Astaire called me on the telephone. He said—these are his exact words—"You're a hell of a mover. Man, you really put them on their asses last night." That's what Fred Astaire said to me. I thanked him. Then he said, "You're an angry dancer. I'm the same way. I used to do the same thing with my cane."

I had met him once or twice in the past, but this was the first time he had ever called me. He went on to say, "I watched the special last night; I taped it and I watched it again this morning. You're a *hell* of a mover."

It was the greatest compliment I had ever received in my life, and the only one I had ever wanted to believe. For Fred Astaire to tell me that meant more to me than anything. Later my performance was nominated for an Emmy Award in a musical category, but I lost to Leontyne Price. It didn't matter. Fred Astaire had told me things I would never forget—*that* was my reward. Later he invited me to his house, and there were more compliments from him until I really blushed. He went over my "Billie Jean" performance, step by step. The great choreographer Hermes Pan, who had choreographed Fred's dances in the movies, came over, and I showed them how to Moonwalk and demonstrated some other steps that really interested them.

Not long after that Gene Kelly came by my house to visit and also said he liked my dancing. It was a fantastic experience, that show, because I felt I had been inducted into an informal fraternity of dancers, and I felt so honored because these were the people I most admired in the world.

Right after *Motown 25* my family read a lot of stuff in the press about my being "the new Sinatra" and as "exciting as Elvis"—that kind of thing. It was very nice to hear, but I knew the press could be so fickle. One week they love you, and the next week they act like you're rubbish.

Later I gave the glittery black jacket I wore on *Motown 25* to Sammy Davis as a present. He said he was going to do a takeoff of me on stage, and I said, "Here, you want to wear this when you do it?" He was so happy. I love Sammy. He's such a fine man and a real showman. One of the best.

I had been wearing a single glove for years before *Thriller*. I felt that one glove was cool. Wearing two gloves seemed so ordinary, but a single glove was different and was definitely a look. But I've long believed that thinking too much about your look is one of the biggest mistakes you can make, because an artist should let his style evolve naturally, spontaneously. You can't *think* about these things; you have to *feel* your way into them.

I actually had been wearing the glove for a long time, but it hadn't gotten a lot of attention until all of a sudden it hit with *Thriller* in 1983. I was wearing it on some of the old tours back in the 1970s, and I wore one glove during the *Off the Wall* tour and on the cover of the live album that came out afterward.

It's so show business that one glove. I love wearing it. Once, by coincidence, I wore a black glove to the American Music Awards ceremony, which happened to fall on Martin Luther King, Jr.'s birthday. Funny how things happen sometimes.

I admit that I love starting trends, but I never thought wearing white socks was going to catch on. Not too long ago it was considered extremely square to wear white socks. It was cool in the 1950s, but in the '60s and '70s you wouldn't be caught dead in white socks. It was too square to even consider—for most people.

But I never stopped wearing them. Ever. My brothers would call me a dip, but I didn't care. My brother Jermaine would get upset and call my mother, "Mother, Michael's wearing his white socks again. Can't you do something? Talk to him." He would complain bitterly. They'd all tell me I was a goofball. But I still wore my white socks, and now it's cool again. Those white socks must have caught on just to spite Jermaine. I get tickled when I think about it. After *Thriller* came out, it even became okay to wear your pants high around your ankles again.

My attitude is if fashion says it's forbidden, I'm going to do it.

When I'm at home, I don't like to dress up. I wear anything that's handy. I used to spend days in my pajamas. I like flannel shirts, old sweaters and slacks, simple clothes.

When I go out, I dress up in sharper, brighter, more tailored clothes, but around the house and in the studio anything goes. I don't wear much jewelry—usually none —because it gets in my way. Occasionally people give me gifts of jewelry and I treasure them for the sentiment, but usually I just put them away somewhere. Some of it has been stolen. Jackie Gleason gave me a beautiful ring. He took it off his finger and gave it to me. It was stolen and I miss it, but it doesn't really bother me because the gesture meant more than anything else, and that can't be taken from me. The ring was just a material thing.

What really makes me happy, what I love is performing and creating. I really don't care about all the material trappings. I love to put my soul into something and have people accept it and like it. That's a wonderful feeling.

I appreciate art for that reason. I'm a great admirer of Michelangelo and of how he poured his soul into his work. He knew in his heart that one day he would die, but that the work he did would live on. You can tell he painted the ceiling of the Sistine Chapel with all his soul. At one point he even destroyed it and did it over because he wanted it to be perfect. He said, "If the wine is sour, pour it out."

I can look at a painting and lose myself. It pulls you in, all the pathos and drama. It communicates with you. You can sense what the artist was feeling. I feel the same way about photography. A poignant or strong photograph can speak volumes.

As I said earlier, there were many changes in my life in the aftermath of *Motown 25*. We were told that forty-seven million people watched that show, and apparently many of them went out and bought *Thriller.* By the fall of

1983 the album had sold eight million copies, eclipsing, by far, CBS's expectations for the successor to *Off the Wall*. At that point Frank Dileo said he'd like to see us produce another video or short film.

It was clear to us that the next single and video should be "Thriller," a long track that had plenty of material for a brilliant director to play with. As soon as the decision was made, I knew who I wanted to have direct it. The year before I had seen a horror film called *An American Werewolf in London,* and I knew that the man who made it, John Landis, would be perfect for "Thriller," since our concept for the video featured the same kind of transformations that happened to his character.

So we contacted John Landis and asked him to direct. He agreed and submitted his budget, and we went to work. The technical details of this film were so awesome that I soon got a call from John Branca, my attorney and one of my closest and most valued advisers. John had been working with me ever since the *Off the Wall* days; in fact he even helped me out by donning many hats and functioning in several capacities when I had no manager after *Thriller* was released. He's one of those extremely talented, capable men who can do anything. Anyway, John was in a panic because it had become obvious to him that the original budget for the "Thriller" video was going to double. I was paying for this project myself, so the money for the budget overruns was coming out of my pocket.

But at this point John came up with a great idea. He suggested we make a separate video, financed by somebody else, about the making of the "Thriller" video. It seemed odd that no one had ever done this before. We felt sure it would be an interesting documentary, and at the same time it would help pay for our doubled budget. It didn't take John long to put this deal together. He got MTV and the Showtime cable network to put up the cash, and Vestron released the video after "Thriller" aired.

The success of *The Making of Thriller* was a bit of a shock to all of us. In its cassette form it sold about a million copies by itself. Even now, it holds the record as the best-selling music video of all time.

The "Thriller" film was ready in late 1983. We released it in February and it made its debut on MTV. Epic released "Thriller" as a single and sales of the album went crazy. According to statistics, the "Thriller" film and the release of the single resulted in fourteen million additional album and tape sales within a six-month period. At one point in 1984, we were selling a million records a week.

I'm still stunned by this response. By the time we finally closed down the *Thriller* campaign a year later, the album was at the thirty-two million mark. Today sales are at forty million. A dream come true.

During this period I changed my management as well. My contract with Weisner and DeMann had expired in early 1983. My father was no longer representing me and I was looking at various people. One day I was at the Beverly Hills Hotel, visiting Frank Dileo, and I asked him if he had any interest in leaving Epic and managing my career.

Frank asked me to think about it some more and if I was certain to call him back on Friday.

Needless to say, I called back.

The success of *Thriller* really hit me in 1984, when the album received a gratifying number of nominations for the American Music Awards and the Grammy Awards. I remember feeling an overwhelming rush of jubilation. I was whooping with joy and dancing around the house, screaming. When the album was certified as the best-selling album of all time, I couldn't believe it. Quincy Jones was yelling, "Bust open the champagne!" We were all in a state. Man! What a feeling! To work so hard on something, to give so much and to succeed! Everyone involved with *Thriller* was floating on air. It was wonderful.

I imagined that I felt like a long-distance runner must

feel when breaking the tape at the finish line. I would think of an athlete, running as hard and as fast as he can. Finally he gets close to the finish line and his chest hits that ribbon and the crowd is soaring with him. And I'm not even into sports!

But I identify with that person because I know how hard he's trained and I know how much that moment means to him. Perhaps a whole life has been devoted to this endeavor, this one moment. And then he wins. That's the realization of a dream. That's powerful stuff. I can share that feeling because I know.

One of the side effects of the *Thriller* period was to make me weary of constantly being in the public eye. Because of this, I resolved to lead a quieter, more private life. I was still quite shy about my appearance. You must remember that I had been a child star and when you grow up under that kind of scrutiny people don't want you to change, to get older and look different. When I first became well known, I had a lot of baby fat and a very round, chubby face. That roundness stayed with me until several years ago when I changed my diet and stopped eating beef, chicken, pork, and fish, as well as certain fattening foods. I just wanted to look better, live better, and be healthier. Gradually, as I lost weight, my face took on its present shape and the press started accusing me of surgically altering my appearance, beyond the nose job I freely admitted I had, like many performers and film stars. They would take an old picture from adolescence or high school, and compare it to a current photograph. In the old picture my face would be round and pudgy. I'd have an Afro, and the picture would be badly lit. The new picture would show a much older, more mature face. I've got a different hairstyle and a different nose. Also, the photographer's lighting is excellent in the recent photographs. It's really not fair to make such comparisons. They have said I had bone surgery done on my face. It seems strange to me that people would jump to that conclusion and I thought it was very unfair.

Judy Garland and Jean Harlow and many others have had their noses done. My problem is that as a child star people got used to seeing me look one way.

I'd like to set the record straight right now. I have never had my cheeks altered or my eyes altered. I have not had my lips thinned, nor have I had dermabrasion or a skin peel. All of these charges are ridiculous. If they were true, I would say so, but they aren't. I have had my nose altered twice and I recently added a cleft to my chin, but that is it. Period. I don't care what anyone else says—it's my face and I know.

I'm a vegetarian now and I'm so much thinner. I've been on a strict diet for *years*. I feel better than I ever have, healthier and more energetic. I don't understand why the press is so interested in speculating about my appearance anyway. What does my face have to do with my music or my dancing?

The other day a man asked me if I was happy. And I answered, "I don't think I'm ever totally happy." I'm one of the hardest people to satisfy, but at the same time, I'm aware of how much I have to be thankful for and I am truly appreciative that I have my health and the love of my family and friends.

I'm also easily embarrassed. The night I won eight American Music Awards, I accepted them wearing my shades on the network broadcast. Katharine Hepburn called me up and congratulated me, but she gave me a hard time because of the sunglasses. "Your fans want to see your eyes," she scolded me. "You're cheating them." The following month, February 1984, at the Grammy show, *Thriller* had walked off with seven Grammy Awards and looked like it was going to win an eighth. All evening I had been going up to the podium and collecting awards with my sunglasses on. Finally, when *Thriller* won for

Best Album, I went up to accept it, took off my glasses, and stared into the camera. "Katharine Hepburn," I said, "this is for you." I knew she was watching and she was.

You have to have some fun.

CHAPTER
SIX

ALL YOU NEED
IS LOVE

had planned to spend most of 1984 working on some movie ideas I had, but those plans got sidetracked. First, in January, I was burned on the set of a Pepsi commercial I was shooting with my brothers.

The reason for the fire was stupidity, pure and simple. We were shooting at night and I was supposed to come down a staircase with magnesium flash bombs going off on either side of me and just behind me. It seemed so simple. I was to walk down the stairs and these bombs would blow up behind me. We did several takes that were wonderfully timed. The lightning effects from the bombs were great. Only later did I find out that these bombs were only two feet away from either side of my head, which was a total disregard of the safety regulations. I was supposed to stand in the middle of a magnesium explosion, two feet on either side.

Then Bob Giraldi, the director, came to me and said, "Michael, you're going down too early. We want to *see* you up there, up on the stairs. When the lights come on, we want to reveal that you're there, so *wait.*"

So I waited, the bombs went off on either side of my head, and the sparks set my hair on fire. I was dancing down this ramp and turning around, spinning, not knowing I was on fire. Suddenly I felt my hands reflexively going to my head in an attempt to smother the flames. I fell down and just tried to shake the flames out. Jermaine turned around and saw me on the ground, just after the explosions had gone off, and he thought I had been shot by someone in the crowd—because we were shooting in front of a big audience. That's what it looked like to him.

Miko Brando, who works for me, was the first person to reach me. After that, it was chaos. It was crazy. No film could properly capture the drama of what went on that night. The crowd was screaming. Someone shouted, "Get some ice!" There were frantic running sounds. People were yelling, "Oh no!" The emergency truck came up and before they put me in I saw the Pepsi executives huddled together in a corner, looking terrified. I remember the medical people putting me on a cot and the guys from Pepsi were so scared they couldn't even bring themselves to check on me.

Meanwhile, I was kind of detached, despite the terrible pain. I was watching all the drama unfold. Later they told me I was in shock, but I remember enjoying the ride to the hospital because I never thought I'd ride in an ambulance with the sirens wailing. It was one of those things I had always wanted to do when I was growing up. When we got there, they told me there were news crews outside, so I asked for my glove. There's a famous shot of me waving from the stretcher with my glove on.

Later one of the doctors told me that it was a miracle I was alive. One of the firemen had mentioned that in most cases your clothes catch on fire, in which case your whole face can be disfigured or you can die. That's it. I had third-degree burns on the back of my head that almost went through to my skull, so I had a lot of problems with it, but I was very lucky.

What we now know is that the incident created a lot of publicity for the commercial. They sold more Pepsi than ever before. And they came back to me later and offered me the biggest commercial endorsement fee in history. It was so unprecedented that it went into *The Guinness Book of World Records.* Pepsi and I worked together on another commercial, called "The Kid," and I gave them problems by limiting the shots of me because I felt the shots they were asking for didn't work well. Later, when the commercial was a success, they told me I had been right.

I still remember how scared those Pepsi executives looked the night of the fire. They thought that my getting burned would leave a bad taste in the mouth of every kid in America who drank Pepsi. They knew I could have sued them and I could have, but I was real nice about it. Real nice. They gave me $1,500,000 which I immediately donated to the Michael Jackson Burn Center. I wanted to do something because I was so moved by the other burn patients I met while I was in the hospital.

Then there was the Victory tour. I did fifty-five shows with my brothers over the course of five months.

I didn't want to go on the Victory tour and I fought against it. I felt the wisest thing for me would be *not* to do the tour, but my brothers wanted to do it and I did it for them. So I told myself that since I was committed to doing this, I might as well put my soul into it.

When it came down to the actual tour, I was outvoted on a number of issues, but you don't think when you're onstage, you just deliver. My goal for the Victory tour was to give each performance everything I could. I hoped people might come to see me who didn't even like me. I hoped they might hear about the show and want to see what's going on. I wanted incredible word-of-mouth response to the show so a wide range of people would come and see us. Word of mouth is the best publicity. Nothing beats it. If someone I trust comes to me and tells me something is great, I'm sold.

I felt very powerful in those days of Victory. I felt on top of the world. I felt determined. That tour was like: "We're a mountain. We've come to share our music with you. We have something we want to tell you." At the beginning of the show, we rose out of the stage and came down these stairs. The opening was dramatic and bright and captured the whole feeling of the show. When the lights came on and they saw us, the roof would come off the place.

It was a nice feeling, playing with my brothers again. It gave us a chance to relive our days as the Jackson 5 and the Jacksons. We were all together again. Jermaine had come back and we were riding a wave of popularity. It was the biggest tour any group had ever done, in huge outdoor stadiums. But I was disappointed with the tour from the beginning. I had wanted to move the world like it had never been moved. I wanted to present something that would make people say, "Wow! That's wonderful!"

The response we got *was* wonderful and the fans were great, but I became unhappy with our show. I didn't have the time or the opportunity to perfect it the way I wanted to. I was disappointed in the staging of "Billie Jean." I wanted it to be so much more than it was. I didn't like the lighting and I never got my steps quite the way I wanted them. It killed me to have to accept these things and settle for doing it the way I did.

There've been times right before a show when certain things were bothering me—business or personal problems. I would think, "I don't know how to go through with this. I don't know how I'm going to get through the show. I can't perform like this."

But once I get to the side of the stage, something happens. The rhythm starts and the lights hit me and the problems disappear. This has happened so many times. The thrill of performing just takes over. It's like God saying, "Yes, you can. Yes, you can. Just wait. Wait till you hear this. Wait till you see this." And the backbeat gets in my backbone and it vibrates and it just takes me. Sometimes I almost lose control and the musicians say, "What is he doing?" and they start following me. You change the whole schedule of a piece. You stop and you just take over from scratch and do a whole other thing. The song takes you in another direction.

There was a part of the show on the Victory tour where I was doing this scatting theme and the audience was repeating what I said. I'd say, "Da, de, da, de" and they'd say, "Da, de, da, de." There've been times when I've done that and they would start stomping. And when the whole audience is doing that, it sounds like an earthquake. Oh! It's a great feeling to be able to do that with all those people—whole stadiums—and they're all doing the same thing you're doing. It's the greatest feeling in the world. You look out in the audience and see toddlers and teens and grandparents and people in their twenties and thirties. Everybody is swaying, their hands are up, and they're all singing. You ask that the house lights come on and you see their faces and you say, "Hold hands" and they hold hands and you say, "Stand up" or "Clap" and they do. They're enjoying themselves and they'll do whatever you tell them. They love it and it's so beautiful—all the races of people are together doing this. At times like that I say, "Look around you. Look at yourselves. Look. Look around you. Look at what you have done." Oh, it's so beautiful. Very powerful. Those are great moments.

The Victory tour was my first chance to be exposed to the Michael Jackson fans since *Thriller* had come out two years earlier. There were some strange reactions. I'd bump into people in hallways and they'd go, "Naw, that can't be him. He wouldn't be here." I was baffled and I'd ask myself, "Why wouldn't I? I'm on earth *somewhere*. I've got to be somewhere at any given time. Why not here?" Some fans imagine you to be almost an illusion, this thing that doesn't exist. When they see you, they feel it's a miracle or something. I've had fans ask me if I use the bathroom. I mean, it gets embarrassing. They just lose touch with the fact that you're like them because they get so excited. But I can understand it because I'd feel the same way if, for instance, I could have met Walt Disney or Charlie Chaplin.

Kansas City opened the tour. It was Victory's first night. We were walking by the hotel pool in the evening and Frank Dileo lost his balance and fell in. People saw this and started to get excited. Some of us were kind of embarrassed, but I was laughing. He wasn't hurt and he looked *so* surprised. We jumped over a low wall and found ourselves on the street without any security. People didn't seem to be able to believe that we were just walking around on the street like that. They gave us a wide berth.

Later when we returned to the hotel, Bill Bray, who has headed my security team since I was a child, just shook his head and laughed as we recounted our adventures.

Bill is very careful and immensely professional in his

job, but he doesn't worry about things after the fact. He travels with me everywhere and occasionally he's my only companion on short trips. I can't imagine life without Bill; he's warm and funny and absolutely in love with life. He's a great man.

When the tour was in Washington, D.C., I was out on our hotel balcony with Frank, who has a great sense of humor and enjoys playing pranks himself. We were teasing one another and I started pulling $100 bills from his pockets and throwing them to people who were walking down below. This almost caused a riot. He was trying to stop me, but we were both laughing. It reminded me of the pranks my brothers and I used to pull on tour. Frank sent our security people downstairs to try and find any undiscovered money in the bushes.

In Jacksonville, the local police almost killed us in a traffic accident during the four-block drive from the hotel to the stadium. Later, in another part of Florida, when the old tour boredom set in that I described earlier, I played a little trick on Frank. I asked him to come up to my suite and when he came in I offered him some watermelon, which was lying on a table across the room. Frank went over to pick up a piece and tripped over my boa constrictor, Muscles, who was on the road with me. Muscles is harmless, but Frank hates snakes and proceeded to scream and yell. I started chasing him around the room with the boa. Frank got the upper hand, however. He panicked, ran from the room, and grabbed the security guard's gun. He was going to shoot Muscles, but the guard calmed him down. Later he said all he could think of was: "I've got to get that snake." I've found that a lot of tough men are afraid of snakes.

We were locked in hotels all over America, just like in the old days. Me and Jermaine or me and Randy would get up to our old tricks, taking buckets of water and pouring them off hotel balconies onto people eating in the atriums far below. We were up so high the water was just mist by the time it reached them. It was just like the old days, bored in the hotels, locked away from fans for our own protection, unable to go anywhere without massive security.

But there were a lot of days that were fun too. We had a lot of time off on that tour and we got to take five little vacations to Disney World. Once, when we were staying in the hotel there, an amazing thing happened. I'll never forget it. I was on a balcony where we could see a big area. There were all these people. It was so crowded that people were bumping into each other. Someone in that crowd recognized me and started screaming my name. Thousands of people began chanting, "Michael! Michael!" and it was echoing all over the park. The chanting continued until finally it was so loud that if I hadn't acknowledged it, it would have been rude. As soon as I did, everybody started screaming. I said, "Oh, this is so beautiful. I've got it so good." All the work I'd put in on *Thriller*, my crying and believing in my dreams and working on those songs and falling asleep near the microphone stand because I was so tired, all of it was repaid by this display of affection.

I've seen times where I'd walk into a theater to see a play and everybody would just start applauding. Just because they're glad that I happen to be there. At moments like that, I feel so honored and so happy. It makes all the work seem worthwhile.

The Victory tour was originally going to be called "The Final Curtain" because we all realized it was going to be the last tour we did together. But we decided not to put the emphasis on that.

I enjoyed the tour. I knew it would be a long road; in the end, it was probably too long. The best part of it for me was seeing the children in the audience. Every night there would be a number of them who had gotten all dressed up. They were so excited. I was truly inspired by the kids on that tour, kids of all ethnic groups and ages. It's been my dream since I was a child to somehow unite people of the world through love and music. I still get goose bumps when I hear the Beatles sing "All You Need Is Love." I've always wished that song could be an anthem for the world.

I loved the shows we did in Miami and all the time we spent there. Colorado was great too. We got to spend some time relaxing up at the Caribou Ranch. And New York was really something, as it always is. Emmanuel Lewis came to the show, as did Yoko, Sean Lennon, Brooke, a lot of good friends. Thinking back, the offstage moments stand out for me as much as the concerts themselves. I found I could lose myself in some of those shows. I remember swinging my jackets around and slinging them into the audience. The wardrobe people would get annoyed at me and I'd say honestly, "I'm sorry but I can't help it. I can't control myself. Something takes over and I *know* I shouldn't do it, but you just can't control it. There's a spirit of joy and communion that gets inside you and you want to just let it all out."

We were on the Victory tour when we learned that my sister Janet had gotten married. Everybody was afraid to tell me because I am so close to Janet. I was shocked. I feel very protective of her. Quincy Jones's little daughter was the one to break the news to me.

I've always enjoyed a wonderfully close relationship with all three of my beautiful sisters. LaToya is really a wonderful person. She's very easy to be around, but she can be funny, too. You go in her room and you can't sit on the couch, you can't sit on the bed, you can't walk on the carpet. This is the truth. She will run you out of her room. She wants everything to be perfect in there. I say, "You *have* to walk on the carpet sometimes," but she doesn't want prints on it. If you cough at the table, she covers her plate. If you sneeze, forget it. That's how she is. Mother says she used to be that way herself.

207

Janet, on the other hand, was always a tomboy. She has been my best friend in the family for the longest time. That's why it killed me to see her go off and get married. We did everything together. We shared the same interests, the same sense of humor. When we were younger, we'd get up on "free" mornings and write out a whole schedule for the day. Usually it would read something like this: GET UP, FEED THE ANIMALS, HAVE BREAKFAST, WATCH SOME CARTOONS, GO TO THE MOVIES, GO TO A RESTAURANT, GO TO ANOTHER MOVIE, GO HOME AND GO SWIMMING. That was our idea of a great day. In the evening, we'd look back at the list and think about all the fun we'd had.

It was great being with Janet because we didn't have to worry that one of us wouldn't like something. We liked the same things. We'd sometimes read to each other. She was like my twin.

LaToya and I are very different, on the other hand. She won't even feed the animals; the smell alone drives her away. And forget going to the movies. She doesn't understand what I see in *Star Wars* or *Close Encounters* or *Jaws.* Our tastes in films are miles apart.

When Janet was around and I wasn't working on something, we'd be inseparable. But I knew we'd eventually develop separate interests and attachments. It was inevitable.

Her marriage didn't last long, unfortunately, but now she's happy again. I do think that marriage can be a wonderful thing if it's right for the two people involved. I believe in love—very much so—how can you not believe after you've experienced it? I believe in relationships. One day I know I'll find the right woman and get married myself. I often look forward to having children; in fact, it would be nice to have a big family, since I come from such a large one myself. In my fantasy about having a large family, I imagine myself with thirteen children.

Right now, my work still takes up most of my time and most of my emotional life. I work all the time. I love creating and coming up with new projects. As for the future, *Que sera, sera.* Time will tell. It would be hard for me to be that dependent on somebody else, but I can imagine it if I try. There's so much I want to do and so much work to be done.

I can't help but pick up on some of the criticism leveled at me at times. Journalists seem willing to say anything to sell a paper. They say I've had my eyes widened, that I want to look more white. More white? What kind of statement is that? I didn't invent plastic surgery. It's been around for a long time. A lot of very fine, very nice people have had plastic surgery. No one writes about their surgery and levies such criticism at them. It's not fair. Most of what they print is a fabrication. It's enough to make you want to ask, "What happened to truth? Did it go out of style?"

In the end, the most important thing is to be true to yourself and those you love and work hard. I mean, work like there's no tomorrow. Train. Strive. I mean, really train and cultivate your talent to the highest degree. Be the best at what you do. Get to know more about your field than anybody alive. Use the tools of your trade, if it's books or a floor to dance on or a body of water to swim in.

Whatever it is, it's yours. That's what I've always tried to remember. I thought about it a lot on the Victory tour.

In the end, I felt I touched a lot of people on the Victory tour. Not exactly in the way I wanted to, but I felt that would happen later, when I was off on my own, performing and making movies. I donated all my performance money to charity, including funds for the burn center that helped me after the fire on the Pepsi set. We donated more than four million dollars that year. For me, that was what the Victory tour was all about—giving back.

After my experiences with the Victory tour, I started making my career decisions with more care than ever. I had learned a lesson on an earlier tour, which I remembered vividly during the difficulties with Victory.

We did a tour years ago with this guy who ripped us off, but he taught me something. He said, "Listen, all these people work for *you*. You don't work for *them*. You are paying them."

He kept telling me that. Finally I began to understand what he meant. It was an entirely new concept for me because at Motown everything was done for us. Other people made our decisions. I've been mentally scarred by that experience. "You've got to wear this. You've got to do these songs. You are going here. You are going to do this interview and that TV show." That's how it went. We couldn't say anything. When he told me I was in control, I finally woke up. I realized he was right.

Despite everything, I owe that guy a debt of gratitude.

Captain Eo came about because the Disney Studios wanted me to come up with a new ride for the parks. They said they didn't care what I did, as long as it was something creative. I had this big meeting with them, and during the course of the afternoon I told them that Walt Disney was a hero of mine and that I was very interested in Disney's history and philosophy. I wanted to do something with them that Mr. Disney himself would have approved. I had read a number of books about Walt Disney and his creative empire, and it was very important to me to do things as he would have.

In the end, they asked me to do a movie and I agreed. I told them I would like to work with George Lucas and Steven Spielberg. It turned out Steven was busy, so George brought in Francis Ford Coppola and that was the *Captain Eo* team.

I flew up to San Francisco a couple of times to visit George at his place, Skywalker Ranch, and gradually we came up with a scenario for a short film that would incorporate every recent advance in 3-D technology. *Captain Eo* would look and feel like the audience was in a spaceship, along for the ride.

Captain Eo is about transformation and the way music can help to change the world. George came up with the name Captain Eo. (*Eo* is Greek for "dawn.") The story is about a young guy who goes on a mission to this miserable planet run by an evil queen. He is entrusted with the responsibility of bringing the inhabitants light and beauty. It's a great celebration of good over evil.

Working on *Captain Eo* reinforced all the positive feelings I've had about working in film and made me realize more than ever that movies are where my future path probably lies. I love the movies and have since I was real little. For two hours you can be transported to another place. Films can take you anywhere. That's what I like. I can sit down and say, "Okay, nothing else exists right now. Take me to a place that's wonderful and make me forget about my pressures and my worries and day-to-day schedule."

I also love to be in front of a 35 mm camera. I used to hear my brothers say, "I'll be glad when this shoot is over," and I couldn't understand why they weren't enjoying it. I would be watching, trying to learn, seeing what the director was trying to get, what the light man was doing. I wanted to know where the light was coming from and why the director was doing a scene so many times. I enjoyed hearing about the changes being made in the script. It's all part of what I consider my ongoing education in films. Pioneering new ideas is so exciting to me and the movie industry seems to be suffering right now from a dearth of ideas; so many people are doing the same things. The big studios remind me of the way Motown was acting when we were having disagreements with them: They want easy answers, they want their people to do formula stuff—sure bets—only the public gets bored, of course. So many of them are doing the same old corny stuff. George Lucas and Steven Spielberg are exceptions.

I'm going to try to make some changes. I'm going to try to change things around someday.

Marlon Brando has become a very close and trusted friend of mine. I can't tell you how much he's taught me. We sit and talk for hours. He has told me a great deal about the movies. He is such a wonderful actor and he has worked with so many giants in the industry—from other actors to cameramen. He has a respect for the artistic value of filmmaking that leaves me in awe. He's like a father to me.

So these days movies are my number one dream, but I have a lot of other dreams too.

In early 1985 we cut "We Are the World" at an all-night all-star recording session that was held after the ceremony for the American Music Awards. I wrote the song with Lionel Richie after seeing the appalling news footage of starving people in Ethiopia and the Sudan.

Around that time, I used to ask my sister Janet to follow me into a room with interesting acoustics, like a closet or the bathroom, and I'd sing to her, just a note, a rhythm of a note. It wouldn't be a lyric or anything; I'd just hum from the bottom of my throat. I'd say, "Janet, what do you see? What do you see when you hear this sound?" And this time she said, "Dying children in Africa."

"You're right. That's what I was dictating from my soul."

And she said, "You're talking about Africa. You're talking about dying children." That's where "We Are the World" came from. We'd go in a dark room and I'd sing notes to her. To my mind, that's what singers should be able to do. We should be able to perform and be effective, even if it's in a dark room. We've lost a lot because of TV. You should be able to move people without all that advanced technology, without pictures, using only sound.

I've been performing for as long as I can remember. I know a lot of secrets, a lot of things like that.

I think that "We Are the World" is a very spiritual song, but spiritual in a special sense. I was proud to be a part of that song and to be one of the musicians there that night. We were united by our desire to make a difference. It made the world a better place for us and it made a difference to the starving people we wanted to help.

We collected some Grammy Awards and began to hear easy-listening versions of "We Are the World" in elevators along with "Billie Jean." Since first writing it, I had thought that song should be sung by children. When I finally heard children singing it on producer George Duke's version, I almost cried. It's the *best* version I've heard.

After "We Are the World," I again decided to retreat from public view. For two and a half years I devoted most of my time to recording the follow-up to *Thriller*, the album that came to be titled *Bad*.

Why did it take so long to make *Bad?* The answer is that Quincy and I decided that this album should be as close to perfect as humanly possible. A perfectionist has to take his time; he shapes and he molds and he sculpts that thing until it's perfect. He can't let it go before he's satisfied; he can't.

If it's not right, you throw it away and do it over. You

work that thing till it's just right. When it's as perfect as you can make it, you put it out there. Really, you've got to get it to where it's just right; that's the secret. That's the difference between a number thirty record and a number one record that stays number one for weeks. It's got to be good. If it is, it stays up there and the whole world wonders when it's going to come down.

I have a hard time explaining how Quincy Jones and I work together on making an album. What I do is, I write the songs and do the music and then Quincy brings out the best in me. That's the only way I can explain it. Quincy will listen and make changes. He'll say, "Michael, you should put a change in there," and I'll write a change. And he'll guide me on and help me create and help me invent and work on new sounds, new kinds of music.

And we fight. During the *Bad* sessions we disagreed on some things. If we struggle at all, it's about new stuff, the latest technology. I'll say, "Quincy, you know, music changes all the time." I want the latest drum sounds that people are doing. I want to go beyond the latest thing. And then we go ahead and make the best record that we can.

We don't ever try to pander to the fans. We just try to play on the quality of the song. People will not buy junk.

They'll only buy what they like. If you take all the trouble to get in your car, go to the record store, and put your money on the counter, you've got to really like what you're going to buy. You don't say, "I'll put a country song on here for the country market, a rock song for that market," and so on. I feel close to all different styles of music. I love some rock songs and some country songs and some pop and all the old rock 'n' roll records.

We did go after a rock type of song with "Beat It." We got Eddie Van Halen to play guitar because we knew he'd do the best job. Albums should be for all races, all tastes in music.

In the end, many songs kind of create themselves. You just say, "This is it. This is how it's going to be." Of course, not every song is going to have a great dance tempo. It's like "Rock with You" isn't a great dance tempo. It was meant for the old dance the Rock. But it's not a "Don't Stop" or "Working Day and Night" rhythm or a "Startin' Something" type of thing—something you can play with on the dance floor and get sweaty, working out to.

We worked on *Bad* for a long time. Years. In the end, it was worth it because we were satisfied with what we had achieved, but it was difficult too. There was a lot of tension because we felt we were competing with ourselves. It's very hard to create something when you feel like you're in competition with yourself because no matter how you look at it, people are always going to compare *Bad* to *Thriller*. You can always say, "Aw, forget *Thriller*," but no one ever will.

I think I have a slight advantage in all of this because I always do my best work under pressure.

"Bad" is a song about the street. It's about this kid from a bad neighborhood who gets to go away to a private school. He comes back to the old neighborhood when he's on a break from school and the kids from the neighborhood start giving him trouble. He sings, "I'm bad, you're bad, who's bad, who's the best?" He's saying when you're strong and good, *then* you're bad.

"Man in the Mirror" is a great message. I love that song. If John Lennon was alive, he could really relate to that song because it says that if you want to make the world a better place, you have to work on yourself and change first. It's the same thing Kennedy was talking about when he said, "Ask not what your country can do for you; ask what you can do for your country." If you want to make the world a better place, take a look at yourself and make a change. Start with the man in the mirror. Start with yourself. Don't be looking at all the other things. Start with *you*.

That's the truth. That's what Martin Luther King meant and Gandhi too. That's what I believe.

Several people have asked me if I had anybody in mind when I wrote "Can't Stop Loving You." And I say that I didn't, really. I was thinking of somebody while I was singing it, but not while I was writing it.

I wrote all the songs on *Bad* except for two, "Man in the Mirror," which Siedah Garrett wrote with George Ballard, and "Just Good Friends," which is by these two writers who wrote "What's Love Got to Do with It" for Tina Turner. We needed a duet for me and Stevie Wonder to sing and they had this song; I don't even think they intended for it to be a duet. They wrote it for me, but I knew it would be perfect for me and Stevie to sing together.

219

"Another Part of Me" was one of the earliest songs written for *Bad* and made its public debut at the end of *Captain Eo* when the captain says good-bye. "Speed Demon" is a machine song. "The Way You Make Me Feel" and "Smooth Criminal" are simply the grooves I was in at the time. That's how I would put it.

"Leave Me Alone" is a track that appears only on the

compact disc of *Bad*. I worked hard on the song, stacking vocals on top of each other like layers of clouds. I'm sending a simple message here: "Leave me alone." The song is about a relationship between a guy and a girl. But what I'm really saying to people who are bothering me is: *"Leave me alone."*

The pressure of success does funny things to people. A lot of people become successful very quickly and it's an instant occurrence in their lives. Some of these people, whose success might be a one-shot thing, don't know how to handle what happens to them.

I look at fame from a different perspective, since I've been in this business for so long now. I've learned that the way to survive as your own person is to shun personal publicity and keep a low profile as much as possible. I guess it's good in some ways and bad in others.

The hardest part is having no privacy. I remember when we were filming "Thriller," Jackie Onassis and Shaye Areheart came to California to discuss this book. There were photographers in the trees, everywhere. It was not possible for us to do anything without it being noticed and reported.

The price of fame can be a heavy one. Is the price you pay worth it? Consider that you really have *no* privacy. You can't really do anything unless special arrangements are made. The media prints whatever you say. They report whatever you do. They know what you buy, which movies you see, you name it. If I go to a public library, they print the titles of the books I check out. In Florida once, they printed my whole schedule in the paper; everything I did from ten in the morning until six at night. "After he did this, he did that, and after he did that, he went there, then he went door to door, and then he . . ."

I remember thinking to myself, "What if I were trying to do something that I didn't happen to *want* reported in the paper?" All of this is the price of fame.

I think my image gets distorted in the public's mind. They don't get a clear or full picture of what I'm like, despite the press coverage I mentioned early. Mistruths are printed as fact, in some cases, and frequently only half of a story will be told. The part that doesn't get printed is often the part that would make the printed part less sensational by shedding light on the facts. As a result, I think some people don't think I'm a person who determines what's happening with his career. Nothing could be further from the truth.

I've been accused of being obsessed with my privacy and it's true that I am. People stare at you when you're famous. They're observing you and that's understandable, but it's not always easy. If you were to ask me why I wear sunglasses in public as often as I do, I'd tell you it's because I simply don't like to have to constantly look everyone in the eye. It's a way of concealing just a bit of myself. After I had my wisdom teeth pulled, the dentist gave me a surgical mask to wear home to keep out germs. I loved that mask. It was great—much better than sunglasses—and I had fun wearing it around for a while. There's so little privacy in my life that concealing a little bit of me is a way to give myself a break from all that. It may be considered strange, I know, but I like my privacy.

I can't answer whether or not I like being famous, but I do love achieving goals. I love not only reaching a mark I've set for myself but exceeding it. Doing more than I thought I could, that's a great feeling. There's nothing like it. I think it's so important to set goals for yourself. It gives you an idea of where you want to go and how you want to get there. If you don't aim for something, you'll never know whether you could have hit the mark.

I've always joked that I didn't ask to sing and dance, but it's true. When I open my mouth, music comes out. I'm honored that I have this ability. I thank God for it every day. I try to cultivate what He gave me. I feel I'm compelled to do what I do.

There are so many things all around us to be thankful for. Wasn't it Robert Frost who wrote about the world a person can see in a leaf? I think that's true. That's what I love about being with kids. They notice everything. They aren't jaded. They get excited by things we've forgotten to get excited about any more. They are so natural too, so unself-conscious. I love being around them. There always seems to be a bunch of kids over at the house and they're always welcome. They energize me—just being around them. They look at everything with such fresh eyes, such open minds. That's part of what makes kids so creative. They don't worry about the rules. The picture doesn't have to be in the center of the piece of paper. The sky doesn't have to be blue. They are accepting of people too. The only demand they make is to be treated fairly—and to be loved. I think that's what we all want.

I would like to think that I'm an inspiration for the children I meet. I want kids to like my music. Their approval means more to me than anyone else's. It's always the kids who know which song is going to be a hit. You see kids who can't even talk yet, but they've got a little rhythm going. It's funny. But they're a tough audience. In fact, they're the toughest audience. There have been so many parents who have come to me and told me that their baby knows "Beat It" or loves "Thriller." George Lucas told me his daughter's first words were "Michael Jackson." I felt on top of the world when he told me that.

I spend a lot of free time—in California and when I'm traveling—visiting children's hospitals. It makes me so happy to be able to brighten those kids' day by just showing up and talking with them, listening to what they have to say and making them feel better. It's so sad for children to have to get sick. More than anyone else, kids don't deserve that. They often can't even understand what's wrong with them. It makes my heart twist. When I'm with them, I just want to hug them and make it all better for them. Sometimes sick children will visit me at home or in my hotel rooms on the road. A parent will get in touch with me and ask if their child can visit with me for a few minutes. Sometimes when I'm with them I feel like I understand better what my mother must have gone through with her polio. Life is too precious and too short not to reach out and touch the people we can.

You know, when I was going through that bad period with my skin and my adolescent growth spurts, it was kids who never let me down. They were the only ones who accepted the fact that I was no longer little Michael and that I was really the same person inside, even if you didn't recognize me. I've never forgotten that. Kids are great. If I were living for no other reason than to help and please kids, that would be enough for me. They're amazing people. Amazing.

I am a person who is very much in control of his life. I have a team of exceptional people working for me and they do an excellent job of presenting me with the facts that keep me up-to-date on everything that's going on at MJJ Productions so that I can know the options and make the decisions. As far as my creativity is concerned, that's my domain and I enjoy that aspect of my life as much or more than any other.

I think I have a goody-goody image in the press and I hate that, but it's hard to fight because I don't normally talk about myself. I am a shy person. It's true. I don't like giving interviews or appearing on talk shows. When Doubleday approached me about doing this book, I was interested in being able to talk about how I feel in a book that would be mine—my words and my voice. I hope it will help clear up some misconceptions.

Everybody has many facets to them and I'm no different. When I'm in public, I often feel shy and reserved. Obviously, I feel differently away from the glare of cameras and staring people. My friends, my close associates, know there's another Michael that I find it difficult to present in the outlandish "public" situations I often find myself in.

It's different when I'm onstage, however. When I perform, I lose myself. I'm in total control of that stage. I don't think about anything. I know what I want to do from the moment I step out there and I love every minute of it. I'm actually relaxed onstage. Totally relaxed. It's nice. I feel relaxed in the studio too. I know whether something *feels* right. If it doesn't, I know how to fix it. Everything has to be in place and if it is you feel good, you feel fulfilled. People used to underestimate my ability as a songwriter. They didn't think of me as a songwriter, so when I started coming up with songs, they'd look at me like: "Who *really* wrote that?" I don't know what they must have thought—that I had someone back in the garage who was writing them for me? But time cleared up those misconceptions. You always have to prove yourself to people and so many of them don't want to believe. I've heard tales of Walt Disney going from studio to studio when he first started out, trying to sell his work unsuccessfully and being turned down. When he was finally given a chance, everyone thought he was the greatest thing that ever happened.

Sometimes when you're treated unfairly it makes you stronger and more determined. Slavery was a terrible thing, but when black people in America finally got out from under that crushing system, they were *stronger*. They knew what it was to have your spirit crippled by people who are controlling your life. They were never going to let that happen again. I admire that kind of strength. People who have it take a stand and put their blood and soul into what they believe.

People often ask me what I'm like. I hope this book will answer some of those questions, but these things might help too. My favorite music is an eclectic mix. For example, I love classical music. I'm crazy about Debussy. *Prelude to the Afternoon of a Faun* and *Clair de Lune*. And Prokofiev. I could listen to *Peter and the Wolf* over and over and over again. Copland is one of my all-time favorite composers. You can recognize his distinctive brass sounds right away. *Billy the Kid* is fabulous. I listen to a lot of Tchaikovsky. The *Nutcracker Suite* is a favorite. I have a large collection of show tunes also—Irving Berlin, Johnny Mercer, Lerner and Loewe, Harold Arlen, Rodgers and Hammerstein, and the great Holland-Dozier-Holland. I really admire those guys.

I like Mexican food very much. I'm a vegetarian, so fortunately fresh fruits and vegetables are a favorite of mine.

I love toys and gadgets. I like to see the latest things

manufacturers have come out with. If there's something really wonderful, I'll buy one.

I'm crazy about monkeys, especially chimps. My chimp Bubbles is a constant delight. I really enjoy taking him with me on trips or excursions. He's a wonderful distraction and a *great* pet.

I love Elizabeth Taylor. I'm inspired by her bravery. She has been through so much and she is a survivor. That lady has been through a lot and she's walked out of it on two feet. I identify with her very strongly because of our experiences as child stars. When we first started talking on the phone, she told me she felt as if she had known me for years. I felt the same way.

Katharine Hepburn is a dear friend too. I was afraid to meet her at first. We talked for a while when I first arrived for a stay on the set of *On Golden Pond,* where I was Jane Fonda's guest. She invited me to have dinner with her the next night. I felt very fortunate. Since then, we have visited one another and remained close. Remember, it was Katharine Hepburn who got me to remove my sunglasses at the Grammy Awards. She's a big influence on me. She's another strong person and a private person.

I believe performers should try to be strong as an example to their audiences. It's staggering what a person can do if they only try. If you're under pressure, play off that pressure and use it to advantage to make whatever you're doing better. Performers owe it to people to be strong and fair.

Often in the past performers have been tragic figures. A lot of the truly great people have suffered or died because of pressure and drugs, especially liquor. It's so sad. You feel cheated as a fan that you didn't get to watch them evolve as they grew older. One can't help wondering what performances Marilyn Monroe would have put in or what Jimi Hendrix might have done in the 1980s.

A lot of celebrities say they don't want their children to go into show business. I can understand their feelings, but I don't agree with them. If I had a son or daughter, I'd say, "By all means, be my guest. Step right in there. If you want to do it, do it."

To me, nothing is more important than making people happy, giving them a release from their problems and worries, helping to lighten their load. I want them to walk away from a performance I've done, saying, "That was great. I want to go back again. I had a great time." To me, that's what it's all about. That's wonderful. That's why I don't understand when some celebrities say they don't want their kids in the business.

I think they say that because they've been hurt themselves. I can understand that. I've been there too.

—Michael Jackson
Encino, California
1988

What one wishes is to be touched by truth and to be able to interpret that truth so that one may use what one is feeling and experiencing, be it despair or joy, in a way that will add meaning to one's life and will hopefully touch others as well.

This is art in its highest form. Those moments of enlightenment are what I continue to live for.

—*Michael Jackson*

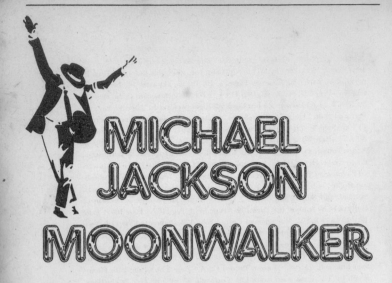